COMPUTE!'s
Quick & Easy
Guide to
HyperCard™

Steven Anzovin

COMPUTE! Publications,Inc.abc

A Capital Cities/ABC, Inc. Company
Greensboro, North Carolina

Dedication
To Rafael and Miriam

Printed in the United States of America

10 9 8 7 6 5 4 3 2

ISBN 0-87455-145-5

The author and publisher have made every effort in the preparation of this book to insure the accuracy of the programs and information. However, the information and programs in this book are sold without warranty, either express or implied. Neither the author nor COMPUTE! Publications, Inc. will be liable for any damages caused or alleged to be caused directly, indirectly, incidentally, or consequentially by the programs or information in this book.

The opinions expressed in this book are solely those of the author and are not necessarily those of COMPUTE! Publications, Inc.

COMPUTE! Publications, Inc., Post Office Box 5406, Greensboro, NC 27403, (919) 275-9809, is a Capital Cities / ABC, Inc. company and is not associated with any manufacturer of personal computers. Finder, *HyperCard*, HyperTalk, ImageWriter, ImageWriter II, ImageWriter LQ, LaserWriter, LaserWriter Plus, Macintosh, Macintosh Plus, Macintosh SE, Macintosh II, *MacPaint, MacWrite, MacDraw*, and Stackware are trademarks of Apple Computer, Inc. *PostScript* is a trademark of Adobe Systems, Inc. *FullPaint* is a trademark of Ann Arbor Softworks. *WriteNow* is a trademark of the T/Maker Company. Direct Drive 20 is a trademark of Jasmine Computer Systems.

Contents

Foreword

Welcome to the future: *HyperCard*, Apple's revolutionary new Macintosh system software and easy-to-use English-language programming environment, is ushering in a new era of computing.

The first Macintosh created a sensation when it was introduced in 1984 because of its revolutionary menu- and icon-based user interface and mouse-driven graphics approach to computing. Now, the revolution continues with the introduction of the remarkable new *HyperCard*, a next-generation breed of software that's rapidly changing the very nature of Macintosh computing.

Designed by Bill Atkinson (the creator of *MacPaint*), *HyperCard* is an extraordinary extension of the user-friendly concept that gives programmers and nonprogrammers alike the tools to make the Macintosh even easier to use. And *COMPUTE!'s Quick & Easy Guide to HyperCard* is your guidebook and reference to this powerful new environment from Apple.

The first half of this book is for all *HyperCard* users, no matter what level your expertise. You'll read about stacks. You'll learn exactly what *HyperCard* is and what it does—why it is the remarkable program that is creating so much excitment.

Learning to navigate though *HyperCard* is easy as you follow the step-by-step instructions presented here. In no time at all you'll be using the stacks that come with *HyperCard*. We've even included easy-to-follow instructions for creating your own stacks.

The latter sections of *COMPUTE!'s Quick & Easy Guide to HyperCard* explore *HyperCard*'s programming language, HyperTalk. HyperTalk is an English-like language that is easy to understand and follow. With its thorough dictionary of HyperTalk, including some previously undocumented commands such as flash, stackSpace, and diskSpace, *COMPUTE!'s Quick & Easy Guide to HyperCard* is *the* clear and concise guidebook you'll want right next to your Mac as you explore the exciting *HyperCard* environment.

Acknowledgments

The author wishes to thank Apple Computer, Inc., and American Business Products of Englewood, New Jersey, for assistance in preparing this book.

Chapter 1
About *HyperCard*

Chapter 1
About *Hypercard*

When the Macintosh was introduced by Apple Computer in 1984, it was hailed as "the computer for the rest of us." Early Macintosh users decided to test Apple's challenge and discovered a powerful computer that was uniquely easy to use. Now Apple is offering another challenge to every new Macintosh owner—an unusual software package called *HyperCard*. According to Apple, *HyperCard* is meant to challenge the way we normally organize and interact with information. In its turn, *HyperCard* is being touted as "the most important development since the Macintosh," "the next step in personal computing," even "programming for the rest of us." Yet there is considerable confusion over what *HyperCard* really is, how to use it, and what to do with it.

What Is *HyperCard*?

Surprisingly, one of the most difficult things about *HyperCard* is describing just what the program is. It's easier to say what the program is not. It is not a typical software application, like a word processor, a database manager, or a paint program (although *HyperCard* can do many of the things that those kinds of programs do). Defining *HyperCard* is difficult because it isn't really just one program, but many.

    HyperCard is. . .

- a vehicle for navigating through knowledge, an "information player." You can use *HyperCard* to search through and display vast amounts of information quickly and easily.
- a relational database. Data and records, text and graphics can be stored in *HyperCard*, related in any way you decide, then printed in a wide variety of formats.
- a full-featured paint program. Included in *HyperCard* is an advanced version of *MacPaint*, the popular graphics program for the Mac, that is always available for customizing the look of your information.

• a construction kit for building software applications. Nonprogrammers will find it easy to devise entirely new ways to organize information for business, education, and entertainment using *HyperCard*'s snap-to-fit programming parts.
• an easy-to-use programming language. *HyperCard*'s powerful scripting language opens fresh avenues of software development to the neophyte programmer.
• a new Macintosh interface, an extension of the Mac's system software. *HyperCard* offers an alternative way to use the Macintosh that does not depend on the Finder. It can connect and control all aspects of the work you do on the Mac.
• a new way to deliver information. Educators, developers, and others will find that *HyperCard* provides an ideal format for teaching and training.
• certain to become an indispensable medium of information exchange for the Macintosh community. Commercial programs are already available that use the *HyperCard* interface or that offer ways to transfer data to and from *HyperCard*. Hundreds of public domain applications that can be used with *HyperCard* have been posted to computer bulletin boards and information exchanges. Apple is committed to supporting *HyperCard* so that it achieves and maintains a central role in Macintosh programming.

You can best understand what *HyperCard* is if you think of it as the jeep, the U.S. Army's old general-purpose vehicle, of Macintosh software. As anyone who owns a jeep can tell you, it doesn't go as fast as a Porsche, ride as smoothly as a Mercedes, or carry as much cargo as a truck. But the jeep can always get you where you want to go—and you can go places with a jeep you just can't go with any other kind of vehicle. You get the same feeling of independence when you work with *HyperCard*. *HyperCard* is sufficiently powerful and adaptable to apply to a wide range of computing tasks, even if it does not possess all the specific features of a dedicated word processor or spreadsheet. In fact, you may abandon many of your stand-alone applications for *HyperCard* applications that you create yourself. Just as you can drive a jeep off the road and into the back country, so you can use *HyperCard* to explore areas of computer programming that no commercial software developer would ever think of going.

How *HyperCard* Works

HyperCard's variant nature is one source of confusion. The theory behind *HyperCard* is also unconventional, and requires some explanation.

At its most basic, *HyperCard* is like a simple card file. All *HyperCard* information is stored on cards, similar in concept to 3 × 5 inch index cards. You can write, draw, and paste clippings on index cards; you can do the same with *HyperCard* cards.

Related cards are grouped together into stacks, much as you would keep paper cards in their own labeled file box or bound together with a rubber band. Whenever you need to find a specific piece of information in your index card file, you thumb through the file and pull out the proper card. Similarly, in *HyperCard*, you can zip through the stack until you reach the card with the information you need. You can organize the cards in your paper index file alphabetically, or by subject, or by any other criteria that you find useful. *HyperCard* allows you to do this, too.

This index card file metaphor breaks down, however, when you consider *HyperCard's* advanced capabilities. For example, *Hypercard's* cards can contain not only words and pictures, but also sounds, music, and animation. You can search for information in *HyperCard* not only by thumbing through cards, but also by specifying the exact information you need, letting *HyperCard* find the right card for you. Information in *HyperCard* can be organized in more than one way at the same time—alphabetically within the stack, say, but also by association and intuition, through reference to related ideas in other stacks. Stacks can be linked together, letting you jump from one body of information to another with just a mouse click. And any number of copies of your *HyperCard* information can be made and shared with your family, friends, and colleagues.

To really understand *HyperCard*, you need to supplement the card file idea with a less familiar concept, *hypermedia*. Most information you encounter is organized hierarchically—one fact after another in a fixed order. A perfect example is your paper index-card file. The cards are in a particular order, and you have to thumb through them one by one to reach the card you want. You could say that the card file information is organized along one dimension—you have to interact with the information in the cards along a line determined by their order. By contrast, hypermedia information is organized along many dimensions and can incorporate every genre of data, including the written and spoken word, pictures, video, and sound recordings.

Each fact in a hypermedia document can be related to every other. You don't have to thumb through the information to locate the fact you want; the hypermedia document can take you to your destination directly because it contains a direct link to that fact. You can think of a hypermedia document as having a structure somewhat like a wheel of Swiss cheese. The holes in the cheese correspond to tunnels or pathways among related information stored in different parts of the document. Instead of having to travel over the surface of the cheese to get to a destination on the other side of the wheel, you use a tunnel to take you right there. (This may be hard to visualize now, but once you start to use *HyperCard*, it will be much easier to understand.) Or you can think of hypermedia as enabling you to "warp" right to the information you need.

Here's an example of how hypermedia (and *HyperCard*) works. Suppose you are reading along in a hypermedia document and you see the word *dsungaripterus*. You want more information on dsungaripterus, so you put the pointer on the word and click. Instantly the screen changes and you are provided with a definition (it's a genus of extinct flying reptile, or pterosaur) and an artist's reconstruction of the beast. You notice that the dsungaripterus's beak structure is unusual for a pterosaur. You click on the beak, and are shown scanned photographs of actual fossil remains. These in turn lead to a scholarly article on pterosaur feeding habits. And so on. In each case, you acquire new information not along an imposed pathway, but by intuition and association, along a route that you determine according to your own interests. Advocates of hypermedia claim that it more closely models the way the human mind works.

HyperCard offers all the power of hypermedia. With *HyperCard*, you can weave words, pictures, sounds, and animation into a multidimensional web of information, a "knowledge-space" that can be explored in a limitless number of ways.

Uses for *HyperCard*

What can you do with *HyperCard?* One obvious use for *HyperCard* is as a personal information organizer. You can, for example, keep a *HyperCard* file of telephone numbers and addresses. Special *HyperCard* features enable you to search through the file instantly for any name and dial any number you select with a click of the mouse. This type of address file is supplied with the program. Other personal uses for *HyperCard* include maintaining files for medical and insurance records; keeping tabs on your software, book, music, or art collections; and scheduling your time.

You can apply the same organizational features to business information. *HyperCard* can function as an infinitely flexible database. With the simple cut-and-paste techniques that all Macintosh software uses, you can re-create in *HyperCard* the paper forms you use in your business now. For instance, you can keep inventory, billing, and employee files in *HyperCard* format. Once in *HyperCard*, your records can be accessed rapidly by any search criteria you specify. More importantly, you can link together the information in the way that is most useful to you. Clicking on a button on your inventory card could instantly take you to another card showing an exploded drawing of the inventoried part or to a card listing alternate suppliers. And you can quickly generate reports in a variety of layouts, selecting only the textual or graphic information you wish to present. While *HyperCard* is not designed or intended to replace high-powered (and high-priced) dedicated relational databases, it can take on many of the information management tasks that small and large businesses must undertake.

Another business use for *HyperCard* is as a tool for creating desktop presentations. The next time you need to present a complex new project, try using *HyperCard* as a slideshow—it has fancy graphics and sound capabilities built right in, including slick video-style transitions. Include line art you create yourself, drawings and photographs digitized with a scanner, or animations designed with other Macintosh programs. The same techniques can be used to devise point-of-sale presentations and storyboards for video and film production.

HyperCard's highly visual approach to portraying information and its point-and-click simplicity make it ideal for training and education. Students can progress through a *HyperCard* lesson at their own pace, absorbing information in screen-size packets. *HyperCard* training can be interactive: The program itself can monitor student responses and tailor the lesson to suit student strengths and weaknesses. For instance, you can program the lesson so that a student who enters a wrong answer is immediately shown a new screen that discusses the problem in more depth. *HyperCard* should be especially attractive to educators because it uses all of the Mac's sophisticated features but is very easy to program.

HyperCard stacks are likely to become a standard method for distributing information to other Macintosh owners. If you have a base of information you want to share, or a commercial product to offer, the *HyperCard* format is a logical vehicle. If you publish product catalogues, for example, you might distribute them as stacks. You needn't worry about the best way to organize your information—simply supply enough links between cards that readers can find what they need with any approach.

The information you distribute need not be factual. *HyperCard* has untapped potential as a medium for artists, writers, and game developers. Imagine *HyperCard* novels, poetry, drama, paintings, animations, puzzles, comics, and adventure games.

Because Apple is bundling *HyperCard* with all new Macintoshes and is making it readily available to everyone else, most Mac owners will have the program and be familiar with its operation. You can distribute your stacks almost like movies are distributed on videocassette, and you can be confident that a large number of users will have the "playback machine," that is, *HyperCard.*

Beginning Your Exploration

This quick-and-easy guide is intended to give you the basic skills you need to use *HyperCard* both as an information player and as a programming tool. *HyperCard* is tailored for both the beginner and the advanced user, and so is this book. Even if you never do more than use *HyperCard* for browsing through stacks designed by others, you'll find some useful hints for navigating your way around the program in the next three chapters. The second part of this book (Chapters 5, 6, and 7) shows you how to use *HyperCard*'s authoring and graphics tools to create and customize your own *HyperCard* applications. And for the advanced *HyperCard* user, Chapters 8 and 9 provide an overview of HyperTalk, *HyperCard*'s easy-to-use programming language. The three appendices contain information on importing and exporting data to and from *HyperCard*, a complete list of keyboard shortcuts, and a glossary of *HyperCard*'s many new terms.

As with all explorations into uncharted territory, you need to adopt an adventurous outlook to get the most from the experience. This book will guide you as you travel, but don't hesitate to experiment for yourself—*HyperCard* has potential that can only be realized by you.

Chapter 2
Getting Started

Chapter 2
Getting Started

Before you start exploring *HyperCard*, be sure you've studied your *Macintosh Owner's Guide* and understand the basic concepts of the Macintosh environment—using the mouse, working with icons, disks, documents and files, and using the Finder. Have a supply of blank 3½-inch disks handy.

Hardware Requirements

HyperCard runs on any Apple Macintosh computer with at least one megabyte of memory, the new 128K or 256K ROM chips, and two 800K disk drives. It's compatible with the Mac Plus, the Mac SE, and the Mac II; it will not run on an older Macintosh 128K or on a 512K (the Fat Mac) computer that has not been upgraded. *HyperCard* supports hard disk drives and add-on displays. (*HyperCard* can only make use of a screen space the size of the original 9-inch-diagonal Macintosh screen, so there will be an unused border around the active *HyperCard* area on larger displays.)

One megabyte of RAM and two floppy drives is the *minimum* hardware configuration. To take full advantage of *HyperCard*'s power to link large amounts of information together, you'll need at least two megabytes of memory and a hard disk drive. *HyperCard* itself requires 250K of memory and tries to control about three times that much. The program's online help system uses 700K more.

You'll find it amazingly easy to fill up a 20-megabyte hard disk with your *HyperCard* information. A 40-megabyte drive or an "infinity drive" with replaceable 10- or 20-megabyte "megafloppies" might be a better choice.

The *HyperCard* Disks

HyperCard comes on four 800K disks. These are:

HyperCard Startup, containing a System folder, the *HyperCard* program, and the *HyperCard* Stacks folder, which includes the Address, Area Codes, Datebook, File Index, Home, Phone, Quotations, and HyperCalc stacks. You can start *HyperCard* directly from this disk.

HyperCard & Stacks, containing duplicates of the *HyperCard* program and of the *HyperCard* Stacks folder, and containing the More Stacks folder, which includes the Book Shelf, Documents, Periodic Table, Plots, and Slide Show stacks. There is no System folder on this or the following two disks.

HyperCard Help, containing the Help Stacks folder, which includes the Help, Help Index, and Help Samples stacks. These stacks provide much basic information on how *HyperCard* works.

HyperCard Ideas, containing the Idea Stacks folder, which includes the Art Ideas, Button Ideas, Card Ideas, Clip Art, and Stack Ideas stacks. Use readymade parts from this disk to create your own *HyperCard* applications.

The disks are not copy-protected, so you can copy them to make backups and to install on a hard disk.

System Software

When you begin work on the Macintosh, you must insert a startup disk into the internal drive (or configure your hard disk to start it automatically). All startup disks, including hard disks, must possess a System file. (The System file contains your computer's basic operating system.) The *HyperCard* Startup disk includes a System folder with a System file in it.

Since the Macintosh was introduced, the System and the Finder (the Mac's disk and file management software) have evolved through many versions. Make sure you're using the proper versions. The *HyperCard* startup disk contains a special version of System 4.1. (No Finder file is necessary on disks that will only be used for *HyperCard*—just a copy of the System file on the *HyperCard* Startup disk.)

On the Macintosh Plus, *HyperCard* will run under System 3.2 and Finder 5.3 or later versions.

On the Macintosh SE, *HyperCard* runs under System 4.0 and Finder 5.4 or later versions.

On the Macintosh II, you'll need System 4.1 and Finder 5.5 or later versions.

If you have an earlier version of the System and Finder, you can get an upgrade to the latest version from your Apple dealer or from a Macintosh user group.

HyperCard and the Macintosh II

In general, *HyperCard* works even faster and smoother on the Macintosh II. However, you should note the following for best results:

- Do not use the special System file that comes on the *HyperCard* Startup disk. Use the System file on the System Tools disk that came with your Mac II.
- Set the screen to two grays (1-bit depth) in the Control Panel's monitor. This will let you see *HyperCard*'s wipes, zooms, and other visual effects.
- *HyperCard* doesn't display in color. You can export cards as *MacPaint* documents and colorize them with various paint programs, but you cannot import color pictures into *HyperCard*.

Backing Up Your Disks

First make backup copies of the *HyperCard* disks on four blank initialized disks and put the originals away in a safe place.

Start your Macintosh with your System Tools disk or any startup disk *except HyperCard* Startup.

Insert a blank disk in the second drive, and initialize it as an 800K disk. Name it *HyperCard Startup Copy.* Repeat this for three more disks, naming them *HyperCard & Stacks Copy, HyperCard Help Copy,* and *HyperCard Ideas Copy.*

Eject the startup disk and insert *HyperCard* Startup in the first drive and *HyperCard* Startup Copy in the second drive. Drag the *HyperCard* Startup disk icon directly over the

HyperCard Startup Copy disk icon. When the System asks you whether you want to copy over the *HyperCard* Startup Copy disk, click on OK. After the disk copy is complete, repeat the procedure with the other disks. At this time you can also initialize a data disk for files you'll be creating; you can label it *WorkStacks*.

   If you have a hard disk, transfer all of the *HyperCard* files to the disk except for the duplicate copies of *HyperCard* and the *HyperCard* stacks folder on the *HyperCard* and Stacks disk. Even if you have a hard disk, it's still a good idea to make floppy disk copies of your originals. Later you may want to delete files from your hard disk that you no longer need.

Starting *HyperCard*

Once you've copied your disks, you can start *HyperCard* by inserting the *HyperCard* Startup disk into the first drive and turning on your Mac. *HyperCard* will load directly, and you can begin work with the program without having to open it from the desktop. (You can think of *HyperCard* as an alternative to the standard Finder user interface.) If you load *HyperCard* Startup into the second drive, simply open the program by clicking on its icon, just as you would any other Macintosh application.

   After you've gained some experience with *HyperCard*, you can create a customized startup disk that contains only the System files, fonts (typefaces), desk accessories, and stacks that you need. The System file on the *HyperCard* Startup disk contains no desk accessories, but it does offer a range of fonts: Chicago 12; Courier 10 and 12; Geneva 9, 10, 12, 14, and 18; Helvetica 10 and 12; Monaco 9; New York 9, 10, 12, 14, and 18; and Times 10, 12, and 18. If you wish to install or remove desk accessories or fonts from your *HyperCard* Startup disk, use the Font/DA Mover on the System Tools disk that came with your computer. (See the *Macintosh Utilities User's Guide* for a discussion of how to use the Font/DA Mover.)

HyperCard Under Multifinder

Multifinder is Apple's new multitasking operating system for
the Macintosh. With Multifinder, you can run more than one
application at a time in separate windows, moving among
them at will without having to close one application and start
another. In some cases, one application can perform work in
the background while you are using another program; for example, you may be able to search for information in *Hyper-
Card* while your spreadsheet recalculates a budget in the
background.

Under Multifinder, *HyperCard* really comes into its own as
a powerful information resource. But you can't run *HyperCard*,
Multifinder, and another application on an ordinary, out-of-
the-box Mac Plus, SE, or II. You'll need at least 2 megabytes of
memory to do that, preferably more. A hard disk drive and an
accelerator board for the Mac Plus and SE are near-necessities.

Many Mac owners use *Switcher*, a utility program that lets
you switch quickly between applications without returning to
the Finder, although it does not permit true multitasking.
HyperCard will work with the latest version of *Switcher*; you'll
need more than 1 megabyte of memory to run any other large
application at the same time.

Saving Your Work

With most Macintosh programs, it is normal practice to save
your work on a regular basis. You must remember to stop
work every 15 minutes or so and consciously save what
you've done by choosing Save or Save As from the File menu.
If you forget to do this, you risk losing the results of your current work session if something unexpected happens, like a loss
of power to the computer. One of *HyperCard*'s most advanced
features is that it does the saving for you automatically. Every
few minutes *HyperCard* will save any work you've done to the
file you have opened, guaranteeing that you'll never lose more
than a few minutes of work. For this reason, however, you
can't run *HyperCard* from a locked or write-protected disk. The
program must be able to write to the disk, including a data
disk, at any time.

Printers and Printer Options

Like all Macintosh applications, *HyperCard* will print out on Apple's ImageWriter II and ImageWriter LQ dot-matrix printers and the LaserWriter and LaserWriter II laser printers. Follow the directions in your printer's manual for hooking up and testing the printer.

You can customize your *HyperCard* startup disk to suit your printer. The System folder on the *HyperCard* startup disk contains only an ImageWriter II printer driver file. This works for the ImageWriter LQ as well. If you own a LaserWriter, you can install a LaserWriter printer driver on the startup disk by moving it over from the System Tools disk. Open the System folders on both disks and drag the LaserWriter icon over to the *HyperCard* disk. Make room on the *HyperCard* disk by throwing the ImageWriter printer driver file into the trash can. (Be sure to keep copies of both drivers on a backup disk.)

LaserWriter owners should note that *HyperCard* will only work with LaserWriter file version 4.0 or higher. Also, *HyperCard* does not output *PostScript* files. *HyperCard* documents only print at the Mac's standard screen resolution of 72 dots per inch, so printouts look exactly like the screen.

Multifinder includes a Background Printing spooler that lets you use the LaserWriter for printing while you work on another application. With *HyperCard*, you will need lots of free disk space for Background Printing a big job, like all the cards in a large stack. This means you'll need a hard disk with at least one megabyte free for the spooling file Background Printing creates.

HyperCard offers a variety of ways to print out information. You can print individual pictures, groups of cards, or text reports. These printing options are covered in more detail in Chapter 4.

Quitting *HyperCard*

Whenever you finish with *HyperCard*, you can quit the program by choosing Quit from the File menu or pressing Command-Q (the Command key is the one with the four-leaf clover on it at the bottom left of the keyboard). If you have used *HyperCard* Startup as your startup disk, choosing Quit will cause your Mac to shut down and eject any disks in the drives. With any other startup disk, including a hard disk, you will return to the desktop.

Chapter 3
HyperCard Navigation

Chapter 3
HyperCard Navigation

Learning how to use a new program is a little like trying to find your way around an unfamiliar country. Sooner or later you come to recognize the major cities and landmarks on your own, but in the beginning it's a lot easier to orient yourself if you have a map. This chapter is your map for navigating the vast terrain of *HyperCard*. You'll visit the prominent landmarks of *HyperCard*, the basic elements that make up the program, and you'll learn to use *HyperCard*'s advanced transportation system for traveling from one element to the next.

The *HyperCard* Elements

Before you begin your exploration of *HyperCard* itself, take a look at Figure 3-1. It shows the *HyperCard* screen and elements—a card, a stack, a field, a button, a menu, a tool, and the message box—and it gives a brief definition of each one. Each element is discussed in detail below. Refer to this figure if you need help in recognizing the various elements or relating them to each other. Now let's take a quick tour through *HyperCard*.

Figure 3-1. The *HyperCard* Elements

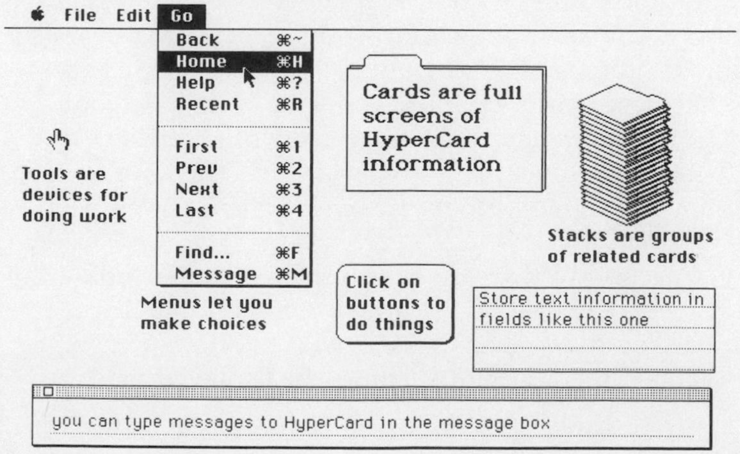

Cards and the Home Card

Switch on your Macintosh and insert the *HyperCard* Startup disk into the first drive and the *HyperCard* Help disk into the second drive. (If you have installed *HyperCard* on a hard disk, double-click on the *HyperCard* icon.) After a moment you'll see the picture illustrated in Figure 3-2.

Figure 3-2. The Home Card

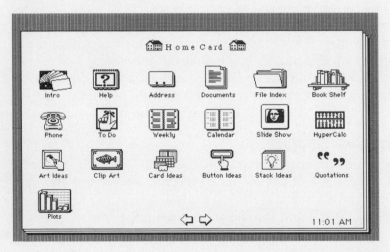

This is a *card*—the fundamental *HyperCard* unit. It's a full screen of *HyperCard* information. Like an ordinary index card, a *HyperCard* card can be read, shuffled, sorted, stacked together with other cards, written and drawn on, created, and thrown away. Unlike an index card, a *HyperCard* card can also play sounds and music, display animation, take you instantly to any related card, ask you questions, and obey your commands. Cards in completely different areas of *HyperCard* can be tied together by links that let you "warp" from one area of the program to another without traversing the intervening distance.

A card occupies the entire *HyperCard* screen, including the area under the menu bar, and it can contain up to 32K of information. You can view and work with only one card at a time. On large-screen monitors, cards are displayed in a

HyperCard window the same size as the standard 9-inch diagonal Macintosh screen (512 × 342 pixels). This window cannot be resized or scrolled, and you cannot display more than one *HyperCard* window at a time.

The card in Figure 3-2 is a special card, called the *Home card.* The Home card displays pictures of the other *HyperCard* areas that are available to you, and it gives you immediate access to any of them by just clicking on a picture. As with any conventional journey, Home is the place to begin and end your travels in *HyperCard.* You can always return to the Home card by choosing Home from the Go menu (see below) or by typing Command-H.

The Menus

If you've used the Macintosh at all, you know how pull-down menus work. Making selections from *HyperCard*'s menus lets you perform common tasks. Pull them down now to take a look at them (see Figure 3-3).

Figure 3-3. The Menus

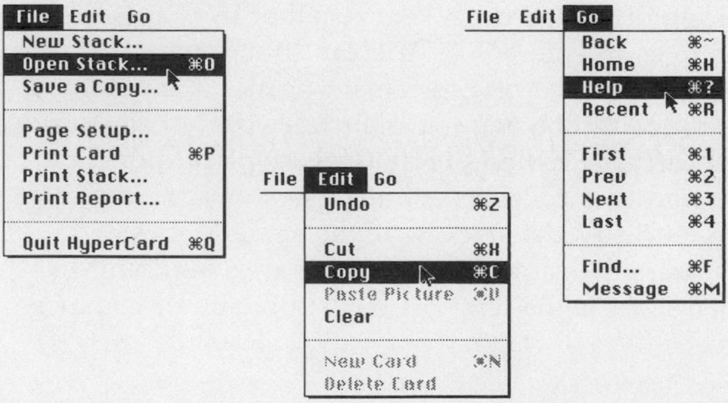

The **File** menu manages *HyperCard*'s files (called *stacks*) and printing operations.

The **Edit** menu lets you perform card and text-editing operations in the usual Macintosh manner.

The **Go** menu is your copilot, giving you the power to move among cards and stacks.

The File and Edit menus should be basically familiar in concept from the Finder and other Macintosh applications. The third menu, Go, will be new to you, but it is the most important in understanding *HyperCard* navigation. We'll return to the Go menu later in this chapter.

One important menu option that you should learn right away is **Undo**, in the Edit menu. Undo negates your most recent action and can be a real lifesaver when you make a mistake or have second thoughts about what you've just done. If you change your mind and want to do what you just undid after all, choose Undo again, and you'll be back where you started. You can also type Command-Z to undo, or press ~ (tilde) or Escape if you are undoing *HyperCard* graphics.

Now is a good time to take a look at *HyperCard*'s online introduction. Click once on the picture labeled *Intro* and follow the instructions. Return to the Home card when you're done.

Stacks

The Home card is actually the first card in the Home *stack*. A stack is a group of related cards kept together in a single *HyperCard* file (as in Figure 3-4). You can think of a stack as the *HyperCard* equivalent of a document or file in another application. There can be many megabytes-worth of cards in a stack. Stacks are usually (but not always) devoted to one theme, for example, a collection of addresses or a picture catalogue. Often all cards in a stack have the same *background*, that is, they share the same general appearance and built-in functions. *Stackware* is the term for public domain or commercial stacks.

Figure 3-4. Stacks Are Made of Cards

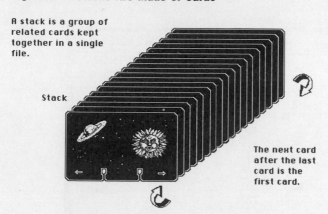

A stack is a group of related cards kept together in a single file.

Stack

The next card after the last card is the first card.

Let's look more closely at a stack. Move the hand pointer over the picture named *Weekly* and click. You'll see Figure 3-5, which is modeled after a page in an ordinary "weekly reminder." You can use the Weekly stack to take notes that can be linked to other stacks, represented by the pictures on the top of the pages. (If you've set the date in the Mac's Control Panel, Weekly should display the pages for the current week when you open it.)

Now click on the right-pointing arrow at the bottom of the right page. Instantly, you'll see the pages for the next week. Actually what you're doing is moving to the next card in the stack. Now click on the left-pointing arrow. The present week is displayed again; you've moved backward one card.

If you continue flipping forward or backward card by card through the stack, you'll see the To Do and Calendar cards (they are part of the same stack), and you'll eventually get back to the Weekly card you started with. Flipping through a stack is like traveling in a circle: You can always return to the place you started by going in one direction long enough. And you can always add a new card to the stack by choosing New Card from the Edit menu or by pressing Command-N. (More about creating cards in Chapters 5, 6, and 7.)

Figure 3-5. The Weekly Card

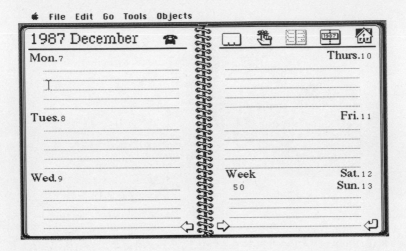

There are several ways to gain access to a stack without having to start from Home.

From the Finder, you can double-click the stack icon.

From any card, you can choose Open Stack from the File menu. You'll see a file dialog box; choose the stack you want to see by double-clicking on its name. If you are looking for a stack in another folder or disk, the Finder may ask you for the disk or folder's location and name.

Many well-designed cards will include links letting you go directly to another stack (an example of this is the house picture on the Weekly card, which takes you directly to the Home card, the first card of the Home stack).

HyperCard saves stacks (and any changes you make to them) to disk automatically. But you can save a duplicate of the stack by choosing Save a Copy from the File menu. Enter a stack name in the save file dialog box (don't use exactly the same name as the original stack's name) and click on Save. It's a good idea to keep backup copies of valuable stacks.

Three stacks you'll be referring to often are *HyperCard*'s Help stacks, found on the *HyperCard* Help disk. These give valuable online assistance and information while you're working with the program. As you are learning about *HyperCard*, keep the Help disk in the second drive (or, if you're using a hard disk, be sure to install Help on the disk). You can always go to Help by choosing Help from the Go menu, clicking on the Help picture in the Home card, or typing Command-? .

Important note: One stack you cannot do without is the Home stack. It must be on the same disk as *HyperCard* itself for the program to work.

Buttons

Return to the Weekly card if you haven't already done so. You'll see several small pictures and symbols on the card. These are *buttons*, areas on cards that you click on to initiate an action, such as going to another card. Buttons link cards and stacks together and make possible the great ease with which you can move about in *HyperCard*. The arrows that you clicked on to flip cards in the Weekly stack are a common type of *HyperCard* button; so are the pictures on the Home card. Other button types are shown in Figure 3-6.

Figure 3-6. The Buttons

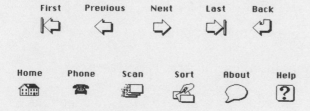

Try clicking on various buttons now to see what they do or where they take you. If you get lost, just return to the Home card to get your bearings.

Fields

Cards also have areas where you can enter text. These are called *fields*. You can type in fields just as you can in a word processor. The hand pointer turns into an *I*-beam cursor when you are passing over an area in a card where you can add or edit text. The ruled areas on the Weekly card are fields. Try typing in one of the text fields now (see Figure 3-7).

Figure 3-7. Typing in a Field

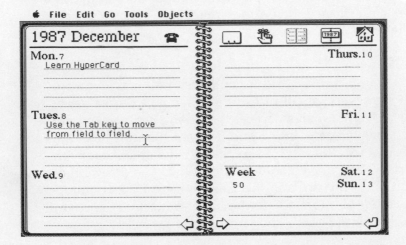

To type in a field:

1. Position the *I*-beam over the first line in the upper left field, and click.
2. You'll see a flashing insertion marker. Type *Learn HyperCard*.
3. You can edit the text using the standard Macintosh editing techniques—selecting text by dragging over it and then cutting, copying, or pasting it. These options are available from the Edit menu (see the discussion of *HyperCard*'s menus, below).
4. To move from field to field on a card, press Tab or click in the next field. Shift-Tab takes you to the previous field.

Note that fields come in different sizes and shapes. Most fields, including the Weekly card fields, have a fixed capacity and cannot display more text than can fit in the field. You'll find, though, that if you keep typing after you've apparently filled the field, text will be added anyway, but outside the visible boundaries of the field. If necessary, use Backspace to eliminate this additional text.

Tools

Tools are devices for doing work in *HyperCard*. There are general tools, which set the stage for performing a particular set of tasks, like browsing or creating new fields and buttons, and more specific tools for creating graphics (more about tools in Chapters 5, 6, and 7). The hand pointer you've been using is the *HyperCard browse tool*, the tool for moving about in the program, clicking buttons, and so on. The browse tool is turned on whenever you enter the program, and it's the one you'll use most often. Only one general tool can be active at a time.

User Preferences

To gain access to the other tools, you must set your *user preferences*. *HyperCard* offers five levels of sophistication, ranging from *browsing*, which limits you to moving about in the program using buttons and the menus, to *scripting*, which allows you to write scripts for entirely new *HyperCard* applications. Each user level adds new capabilities to those available in the previous level; you needn't move up to a new set of capabilities until you are ready.

Browsing is the lowest level; it limits you to moving about and finding information using the browse tool.

Typing, the second level, adds the capability of typing in fields and issuing commands to *HyperCard* in a special window, the message box (see below).

Painting gives you access to *HyperCard*'s *MacPaint*-like painting tools for drawing pictures and customizing cards.

Authoring adds stack, card, button, and field designing tools and menu options.

Scripting incorporates everything in the other levels and also allows you to write *HyperCard* scripts in HyperTalk, *HyperCard*'s programming language.

To set the user level you want from the User Preferences card in the Home stack:

1. Return Home by clicking the house picture in the Weekly card, by choosing Home from the Go menu, or by typing Command-H.
2. Choose Last from the Go menu. You'll go to the last card in the Home stack, which is the User Preferences card. It's shown in Figure 3-8.

Figure 3-8. User Preferences Dialog Box

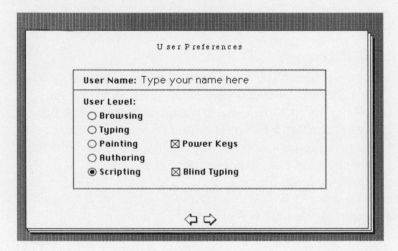

3. Type in your name; then choose one of the levels by clicking on its button.
4. The user level is preset to typing. This is fine if all you plan to do is use stackware or the stacks already supplied with *HyperCard*. To get the most out of the program, however, you should select the highest level, scripting. This book assumes you're ready to tackle *HyperCard*'s higher functions; click on the scripting button and on the blind typing and

power keys check boxes. These will all be dealt with in later chapters.

5. Click on the right arrow button to return to the Home card.

The Expanded Menus

Now that you've set the user level to scripting, you'll see that two new menus have been added, Tools and Objects. If you pull down the other menus, you'll also see that new commands have been added to the File and Edit menus. Figure 3-9 shows how File and Edit look at the scripting user level.

Figure 3-9. The Expanded File and Edit Menus

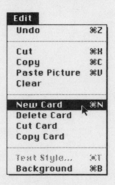

The **Tools** menu contains the general tools for browsing and creating buttons and fields, plus *HyperCard*'s painting tools. The Tools menu is a new kind of Macintosh menu. It can be "torn off" the menu bar and placed anywhere on screen. This is accomplished by pulling down the menu and then dragging it by a bottom corner. The menu detaches and can be dragged wherever you need it, just like an ordinary Mac window.

The **Objects** menu works in conjunction with the Tools menu to help you customize cards and create new applications. It provides detailed information on all the *HyperCard* elements. Figure 3-10 illustrates the Tools and Objects menus.

Figure 3-10 The Tools and Objects Menus

Later chapters will cover the many menu options you see here, as well as others that only become visible when a tool is selected. For the moment, you only need to be familiar with the File, Edit, and Go menus. (See Appendix B for a summary of the keyboard shortcuts for *HyperCard* menu commands.)

Moving from Card to Card with the Go Menu

The Go menu is the one you'll be using most often at this stage. Return to the Weekly stack and take a moment to try out each Go command.

Back (Tilde, Esc, or the down arrow) moves you back to the last card you viewed.

Home (Command-H) takes you home.

Help (Command-?) moves you to the first card in the Help stack.

Recent (Command-R) is a special feature that shows you miniature pictures of the 42 cards you've visited most recently. Figure 3-11 shows the Recent card. You can go to any of these cards by clicking on its miniature (which is really a button). Click on the card picture with the box around it or type *Return* to go to the last card you looked at. Recent is especially helpful when you want to return to a particular card but can't remember what stack it is in or how to get there.

Figure 3-11. Recent

File   Edit   **Go**   Tools   Paint   Options   Patterns

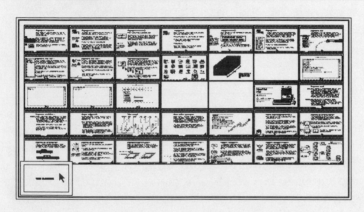

First (Command-1 or Command-Left Arrow), **Prev** (Command-2 or Command-Left Arrow), **Next** (Command-3 or Command-Right Arrow), and **Last** (Command-4 or Command-Right Arrow) take you to specific cards in the stack you're currently looking at.

For example, the User Preferences card is the last one in the Home stack; you can get there by clicking on the right-pointing arrow at the bottom of the Home stack cards until you reach the User card, but it's faster to just choose Last from the menu. First takes you to the first card in the stack; Prev takes you to the previous card in the stack (as distinct from Back, which takes you to the last card you viewed); and Next goes to the next card, cycling you to the first card in the stack if you're at the last card.

Find and **Message** give you the ability to do text searches in the current stack and to issue typed commands to *HyperCard*. We'll explore these features next.

The Message Box

Choose Message or type Command-M to see the *message box*,
a small window that appears at the bottom of the screen. Use
the message box to issue commands to *HyperCard*. Type these
commands into the message box, pressing Return or Enter
after each one. Each new command will erase the one before
it. Or, you can select it and press Return or Enter, or backspace over individual letters.

- go to the first card of address
- go last
- the date
- show cards

As you can see, the message box is another way to navigate in *HyperCard*. To go in any direction or to any available
stack, just type *Go* and the direction or stack name. You can
also use the message box to get information from *HyperCard*,
as you did when you asked for the date, or to perform a simple action, like showing all cards in the stack. (Incidentally,
you've just used HyperTalk, *HyperCard*'s programming language. HyperTalk is the subject of Chapters 8 and 9.)

A note on message box syntax: There are several ways to
frame commands to the message box. For example, if you
want to be taken to the Home stack, you can type any of the
following:

Go to the First Card of the Home Stack
Go to card 1 of home
Go stack "home"
Go home

All of these will take you to the Home card, which is the
first card of the Home stack. (*HyperCard* will always take you
to the first card of a requested stack unless you tell it otherwise.) *HyperCard* is very understanding; it usually knows what
you want to do even if you say it in more than one way. Generally, though, you'll save time if you give the shortest form of
the command. Here are some common message box commands and the most efficient format for each.

Go

Form: go [stack or card name or description]
            Takes you to the specified stack or card.
Examples: go back
            go datebook
            go card 4 of address

DoMenu

Form: doMenu [menu option]
            Performs the specified menu option.
Examples: doMenu recent
            doMenu print card
            doMenu save a copy. . . (make sure to type in the
            ellipses)

Open

Form: open [application] [application with document]
            Opens the named application and document. Be sure to
            specify the *pathname* for the document and application on
            the Documents cards in the Home stack (see Chapter 4
            for a discussion of how to do this).
Examples: open MacDraw
            open letter with WriteNow
            open geisha with MacPaint

Push Card

Form: push card
            Tags the current card for easy retrieval. Go to a pushed
            card at any time by using pop card (see below). You can
            push as many cards as you like.

Pop Card

Form: pop card
            Retrieves any pushed cards in reverse order (last-pushed,
            first-popped). Popped cards must be retagged with a
            push card command before they can be popped again.

Show Cards

Form:　　　show [cards] [all cards] [number] of cards
　　　　　　Show cards shows all cards in the stack in quick succes-
　　　　　　sion, cycling continually until you click the mouse. Show
　　　　　　all cards cycles through the stack cards once. Show [num-
　　　　　　ber of] cards flashes only the number of cards you ask
　　　　　　for, beginning with the card after the current card.

Examples:　show cards
　　　　　　show all cards
　　　　　　show 10 cards

Date

Form:　　　the date; the long date
　　　　　　The date gives the current month/day/year in numeral
　　　　　　form; the long date yields the date fully spelled out.

Examples:　the date (returns "11/2/87")
　　　　　　the long date (returns "Monday, November 2, 1987")

Time

Form:　　　the time, the long time
　　　　　　The time yields the current hour and minute in numeric
　　　　　　form. The long time adds seconds.

Examples:　the time (returns "11:15 AM")
　　　　　　the long time (returns "11:15:56 AM")

The message box also works as an algebraic calculator, complete with a full range of mathematical operators and functions including exponents, trigonometric functions, and pi. Try these, pressing Return to execute the calculations:

5 + (2 / 7)
(5 + 2) / 7
2 * pi
12 ^ 2
12 ^ 3
sin(60)
sqrt(625)

The symbol * means times or multiplied by; / means divided by; ^ means to the power of (12 ^ 3 is 12 to the third power, or 12 cubed); **sqrt** is the square root.

Like a normal Macintosh window, the message box can be moved anywhere on the screen by dragging it by the gray bar along its top. Close it by clicking on the close box at the upper left corner. Type *test* into the message box and close it now. Then choose Message again from the Go menu. The message box reappears, with "test" still entered. The message box remembers whatever you last entered and displays the text again when you reopen it, ready for further editing. And, you can type a message to the message box even if it isn't visible. Just make sure that the Blind Typing box is checked on the User Preferences card.

Searching for Text

One of *HyperCard*'s most useful features is its ability to perform very rapid text searches. Using the message box, you can ask *HyperCard* to find any word or combination of words in a text field anywhere in a stack. For example, a text search is the quickest way to find the phone number of a business contact on a card in the Address stack (just tell *HyperCard* the name, and it will find the right card for you), or a keyword (like *meeting*) in the Weekly stack.

To perform a text search:

1. Go to the Phone stack (there's a button that takes you to Phone on the Home card) and click on the Area Codes button. You'll see a card listing area codes for major U. S. cities in one region.
2. Now choose the Find command in the Go menu (or type Command-F). The message box reappears, this time with the command Find already typed in and followed by open and close quotation marks. Any text you're trying to find must be enclosed by quotation marks, though *HyperCard* doesn't care about other things, like capitalization. You can search for any three-letter combination, a complete word, a line of words, or words in a specified field.

3. Type "Brooklyn" (inside quotation marks) and press Return. You'll see a spinning beachball, letting you know that *HyperCard* is performing the search. Within a second or two you'll see the 718 area-code card, with the word "Brooklyn" in a box.

4. Now look for New York City. Backspace over "Brooklyn" and type "New York" (press Return). *HyperCard* now finds the first occurrence of both "new" and "york" in any order on a card in the stack. If you keep pressing Return, you'll be taken to every "new" in the stack, whether it belongs to New York, Newark, or New Rochelle, as long as the letter combination "york" is also somewhere on the card. There are nine cards in all with "new" and "york" on them, even though the city has only one area code (212). Obviously, it pays to be as specific as possible when doing a search. Typing "New York City" into the message box narrows the search considerably, since that combination of words appears on only three cards in the stack.

5. Delete the space between "new" and "york" in the message box ("newyork") and press return. You'll hear a beep—that means that *HyperCard* can't find the combination of letters you've specified. If that happens, always check your spelling before trying another search word.

You can search for other occurrences of text that already appears in a field by choosing Find and then dragging over the text while pressing the Command key. The selected text will automatically appear in the message box. This works for up to a line of text. Stop a search in progress by pressing Command-. (period).

Now you've mastered the skills you need for *HyperCard* navigation. In the next chapter, we'll look in more detail at the stacks supplied with *HyperCard*.

Chapter 4
Exploring *HyperCard* Stacks

Chapter 4
Exploring *HyperCard* Stacks

The four *HyperCard* disks come with a rich assortment of stacks and ideas that you can apply immediately to your own work. In this chapter, we'll take a look at the set of integrated desk utilities included on the *HyperCard* Startup and *HyperCard* & Stacks disks, as well as at methods for printing and protecting your cards and stacks. As you learn to use the supplied stacks, you'll also be delving into some of the deeper areas of *HyperCard* you haven't yet encountered.

The Addressbook

The Addressbook (Figure 4-1) functions in much the same way as the address and phone-number file you now keep on your desk near the phone. Like your paper address file, you can change the information on the Addressbook's cards, add new cards as you need them, and throw away cards you no longer need; but the Addressbook also offers some significant

Figure 4-1. The Addressbook

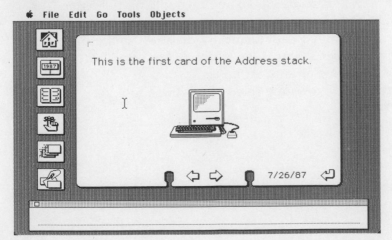

enhancements. Go to the Addressbook now by clicking on the Address button on the Home card and take a look at the sample cards.

An Address card contains familiar fields where you enter text; the standard arrows for moving back and forth among cards, several buttons along the left for special functions, and an open message box. Choose New Card from the Edit menu (or enter Command-N) whenever you want to extend your Addressbook. You'll get a fresh card with all the same attributes and features.

Fields. The Addressbook's text fields are all in the index card part of the card. There are three text fields, but notice that there is no indication of exactly where or how big those fields are.

To find out the location and size of the fields:

1. Go to the second card in the stack.
2. Pull down the Tools menu. Along the top you'll see the icons for *HyperCard*'s three general tools: the browse tool, the button tool, and the field tool.
3. Select the field tool (the one on the right).
4. The card's three fields will suddenly pop into view, displaying their exact size and location and how many lines of text you can put into them with the current font (see Figure 4-2). In the main field at the top, there is enough room to enter a name (make sure to put the name alone on the top line if you plan to sort the cards) and a couple of addresses. The middle field is for phone numbers; you can fit three. (The Phone button will automatically dial the number in the top line of the second field; see below.) The small bottom field holds the date or another note.
5. To return to browsing, select the browse tool.

Figure 4-2. Addressbook Fields

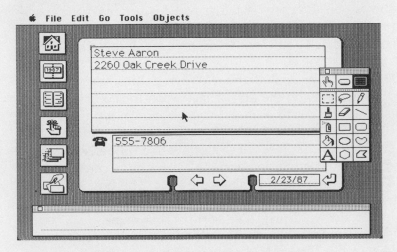

Buttons. Links to Home, the Calendar, the Weekly reminder, and the To Do list are provided by the buttons along the left. Clicking on these will take you to the relevant stack. There are three other buttons that are probably unfamiliar to you:

Scan or View. The button with "speeding cards" (fifth from the top) is the scan (or view) button. It cycles once through all the cards in the stack at top speed for a quick visual search. Try the scan button now. Click again to stop the search at any card.

Sort. The button at bottom left is the sort button. Click on it now. A dialog box will ask you if you wish to sort your cards alphabetically by first or last name. When you choose a sort option, *HyperCard* will reorder all cards in the stack to suit.

You may be wondering why a sort button is necessary. After all, when you make a new paper card for you desk index file, you simply insert in into its proper place. *HyperCard* doesn't work that way. When you create a new card, *Hyper-Card* inserts it into the stack *after* the card you are currently

45

viewing—whether it follows in alphabetical order or not—then shows you the new card. The sort feature makes it possible to make a new card wherever you happen to be in the Addressbook stack and then has *HyperCard* automatically put it into place.

Sort does have its limitations. What it does, more precisely, is sort cards by the first or last word in the first line of the first field. Be aware of this if you like to list names last name first (for example, Ames, Russell). Also note that you'll have some cards that just won't alphabetize properly under the last name option. If you sort by last name, a card for Apple Computer, Inc. will alphabetize by *Inc*. The best system is to enter personal names last name first and company names most important word first, then sort by first name.

Phone. The Phone button automatically dials a specified number if your Macintosh is connected to a modem or an acoustic coupler.

To automatically dial a number:

1. Create a new card.
2. Enter a phone number in the first line of the second field.
3. Click on the Phone button.
4. You'll go to the Phone Setup card and the number on the Addressbook card is dialed according to the Phone Setup specifications (see below for how to work with the Phone Setup card).

If there's no number on the Addressbook card, *HyperCard* will display a dialog box asking for one. If there is more than one number (a work and a home number, for example), select the number you want by dragging over it and then clicking the Phone button.

Message Box. The message box is displayed for convenience. Use Find to search for a particular card (try searching for *Walthrop* in the sample cards).

Area Codes and Phone Setup

These linked utility stacks will speed your telephone chores.

Area Codes

The Area Code stack is accessible from the Finder (double-click the Area Codes icon), from the Phone Setup card (click the Area Codes button), or by typing *go area codes* into the message box. It's shown in Figure 4-3.

Figure 4-3. Area Codes

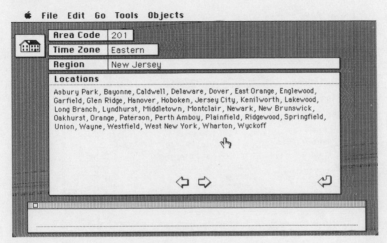

You've worked with Area Codes briefly already, and you may have noticed how it works: Each card lists major cities in one area code, and the cards in the stack are sorted numerically by the area code number. You've probably also noticed that you can't edit the text on these cards—distinctly unfair if your home town isn't listed on the proper card.

To edit the area code cards:

1. Select the field tool in the tools menu.
2. Click in the field that contains the cities to select it. The field will be outlined with a selection box, somtimes called a *marquee*.
3. Pull down the Objects menu and select Field Info. A dialog box pops onscreen with all kinds of information on the field: its name, ID number, style, and so on (see Figure 4-4). Don't worry—we'll be looking at all these new aspects of fields in the next chapter; for now, just note that this field is

a *background field,* meaning that it is common to all similar cards in the Area Codes stack, and that the Lock Text check box has been checked. That means you've been barred from changing any text in the field. Click on the check box to unlock the text, then click OK. Because this field is common to all the cards in the stack, unlocking the field on this card unlocks the same field on all the cards.

Figure 4-4. Unlock Text

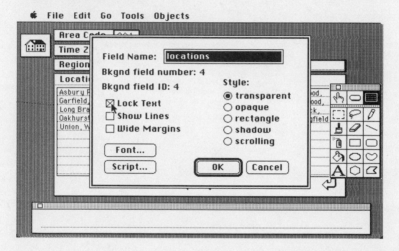

4. Reactivate the browse tool. You can now edit the text in any field on the card, adding or eliminating cities as you please. Since the Area Code stack is a very handy reference—how many times have you had to call 411 for an area code?—it's well worthwhile to add cities you're likely to call. You can also use the same stack to list international calling codes. Just create a new card and enter the proper information in the relevant fields. Sorting the Area Code cards is not particularly important, since you'll be using Find for any searches of the stack.

Phone Setup

The Phone Setup card (Figure 4-5) will autodial any number you specify as long as your Macintosh is connected to a modem or an acoustic coupler. Go to Phone Setup via the Phone button on the Home, Addressbook, Calendar, Weekly Reminder, To Do, and Area Codes cards; or type *Go phone* into the message box. Phone Setup's special features include text fields for entering phone numbers, quick access to the Area Codes stack with a button, and buttons for entering modem type and initiating autodialing.

Figure 4-5. The Phone Setup

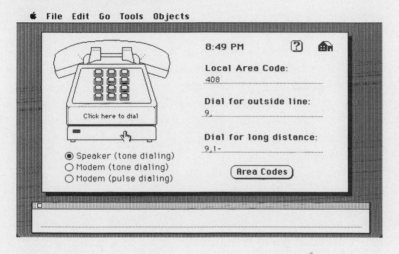

First look at the fields on the right. (You might want to examine them with the field tool on.) These are for entering preambles, telephone prefixes such as area codes, easy access numbers, outside-line numbers, and any codes you need to add to operate your modem. Any characters entered in these fields will be automatically added to the number you want to dial, depending on whether you are dialing a long-distance or local number. *HyperCard* looks for an area code in front of the number and, if it finds one, will add an easy-access or other preamble. Otherwise, the program assumes you are dialing a local number. Edit the numbers already typed in as necessary.

At the right is a large picture of a telephone labeled *Click Here to Dial*. It's hard to know just what location is meant by "here." Luckily you can find out detailed information on buttons the same way you can with fields.

To find out information on buttons:

1. Open the Tools menu and select the Button tool.
2. All the buttons on the card will be outlined, including the entire phone graphic, which is a very large button. You can click anywhere on the phone to initiate dialing.
3. Reselect the browse tool.

To use Phone Setup for dialing:

1. Connect your modem or coupler and turn it on.
2. Go to the Phone Setup card.
3. Select the proper modem setting, if required.
4. Enter a number into the message box by typing it in or pasting from another card. You don't need to add parentheses or a dash to separate an area code or easy access code from the local exchange, just type a string of numbers. For example, (10652-1-201) 774-2369 can be entered 1065212017742369.
5. Hit Return or Enter and click on the Phone button.
   HyperCard will dial the number.

The Datebook

The linked Calendar, Weekly reminder, and To Do list (which we'll now call the *Datebook*) are familiar from Chapter 3. Having these three together in one stack makes an easy-to-use planning tool, one that effectively mimics the paper datebook that many people carry with them. But there are a few aspects to *HyperCard*'s Datebook that you may not have discovered yet.

To learn more about the Datebook:

1. Go to the Calendar (see Figure 4-6) by clicking on the Calendar button in the Home card or any linked card. It extends through the end of 1989. Flip to the current week and click on today's date. Instantly, you'll zoom to the corresponding page in the Weekly reminder. When you return to the Calendar, the current week will be boxed.

Figure 4-6. The Calendar

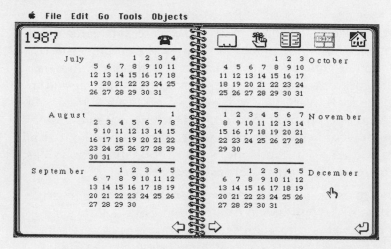

2. Go to the end of the Weekly part of the stack. The last
   Weekly page contains an Extend button that will make up
   six months of new cards on command. Note how this is different from simply creating a new card with New Card from
   the File menu: Those would not contain any dates. Try New
   Card to see the difference. You can drop cards from Weekly
   at any time with an option in the File menu. Go to the card
   you want to delete, then select Delete Card. This can be
   worthwhile if the stack is getting too large. Be sure to print
   out a copy for your records (see the section on printing,
   below).

   Phone numbers you jot down on the To Do or Weekly
   cards can be dialed automatically by selecting them and then
   clicking on the Phone button.

Document Representatives

This utility stack, located in the More Stacks folder on the *HyperCard* and Stacks disk, helps you create data cards on all your applications, stacks, and other files. Assembling information on all your documents can be a vital help if you are using a hard disk with many files, if you have files nested in multiple folder layers, or if you routinely transfer different file types from one program to another. Document Representative cards provide much the same kind of information about applications and files that the Finder's Get Info menu option does.

To create Document Representative cards:

1. If you're using two floppy drives, open *HyperCard* in drive 1 and the disk you want to catalogue in drive 2. Make sure the Documents card is on the disk you want to catalogue.
2. Open the Documents stack (it's just one card; see Figure 4-7) by clicking on the Documents button on the Home card.

Figure 4-7. The Document Rep Card

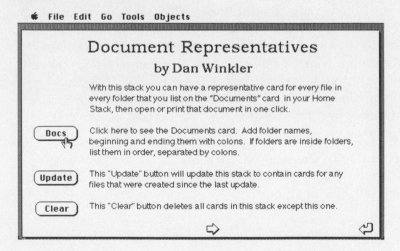

52

3. Click on the Documents button. This takes you to the "Look for Documents In" card in the Home Stack.
4. Enter the names of any disks and folders that contain files you want cards for; remember to add colons before and after folder names.
5. Go to the previous card and enter names of applications you want listed. Enter names of stack folders on the card before that one. It's important to list all your documents and applications on these cards, because they provide the information *HyperCard* needs to open them with the Open command.
6. Return to the Documents Representatives card via Home, Recent, or the message box.
7. Click on the Update button. *HyperCard* will create a card for each file; a sample card is shown in Figure 4-8. It includes important information such as the type, size, and creation date of files and stacks. You can open stacks, applications, and non-*HyperCard* files; and you can print files and pictures by clicking on the buttons at the upper right. When you quit an external file or application, you'll be returned automatically to the last *HyperCard* card you were working with. Printing out the Document Representative cards themselves is also a good idea, so you can have a reference to all your files even when you're not working with *HyperCard*.

Figure 4-8. Sample File Representative Card

    File   **Edit**   **Go**   **Tools**   **Objects**

Name: Documents
Where: :HyperCard Stacks:
Type: STAK   **Creator**: WILD   **Size**: 20 K   Print   Open
Created: Saturday, July 4, 1987   **Modified**: Friday, December 11, 1987
Notes:

Printing Cards and Reports

In the electronic age, paper documents are more important than ever. You'll often want to create printed copies of the information you've stored in *HyperCard*. *HyperCard* offers a rich variety of printing options.

Page Setup. The Page Setup dialog box lets you set the basic parameters for printing: page orientation and size, special effects, and so on. The ImageWriter Page Setup box is shown in Figure 4-9. Be sure to set your choices here before printing anything in *HyperCard*.

Figure 4-9. ImageWriter Page Setup

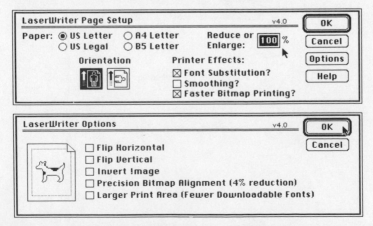

The LaserWriter Page Setup box (Figure 4-10) offers more options, including flipped and negative images and smoothing for graphics. Generally, settings you use with other Macintosh programs, especially graphics programs, will work well for *HyperCard*, with the following caveats and notes:

Figure 4-10. LaserWriter Page Setup and Options

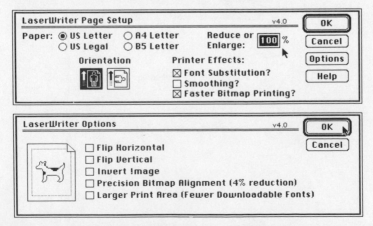

• Reduced or enlarged printing doesn't work with *HyperCard*.
• Font Substitution replaces a screen font with a similar laser
  font. This may create word spacing problems, but it also pro-
  vides higher-resolution letters.
• Smoothing smooths out the jagged edges of Macintosh
  graphics to some degree, but it slows printing considerably.
  So do the flipping and Invert options.
• Choose Faster Bitmap Printing if you are using Horizontal
  Orientation. Turn it off when using the Invert option.
• Precision Bitmap Alignment compensates for the difference
  between the Mac's 72-dot-per-inch (dpi) resolution and the
  LaserWriter's 300 dpi resolution to yield slightly less dis-
  torted graphic images.
• Larger Print Area lets you use more of the total page, but it
  leaves less memory for downloadable fonts.

Print Card. Any card can be printed using the Print Card
option in the File menu or by typing Command-P. Turn on
your printer, select Print Card, and you'll get a printout of the
entire current card.

Print Stack. You have many options when you want to
print the actual appearance of all the cards in a stack. Make
sure you are using a general tool (the browse, button, or field
tool), then choose Print Stack from the File menu to see the
Print Stack dialog box (Figure 4-11).

Figure 4-11. Print Stack Dialog Box

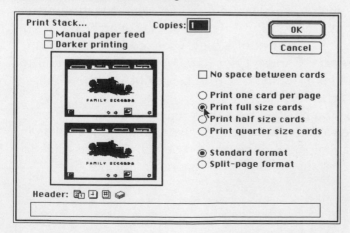

This will let you print 1 card per page, or 2 (full-size), 8 (half-size), or 32 (quarter-size) cards per page. The page layout window in the dialog box shows you roughly what each choice will look like. Toggle back and forth among the choices to get a feel for each page layout. Half-size cards are just legible with an ImageWriter, but the quarter-size format yields unreadable cards with an ImageWriter and should only be used with a LaserWriter. The more cards per page, however, the faster the stack will print.

Choose Standard Format if you plan to bind the stack printout in a standard three-ring binder. Split-page Format leaves a horizontal gutter margin in the middle so that you can fold the printouts in half and bind them in a 5½ X 8½ inch executive organizer or minibinder. Toggle between these options to see how they affect page layout.

Add a header to each page with the header box at bottom. You can also add the time, date, page number, and stack name to the Header by positioning the text pointer and selecting the appropriate icons (don't forget to add spaces between them). The header is shown in the page layout window.

Once you've set these printing parameters, *HyperCard* will print the stack by those parameters until you change them. You might try out stack printing by printing the Clip Art stack on the Ideas disk.

Print Report. Often you won't want to print out graphic images of the cards in a stack, but only the textual information the cards contain. With *HyperCard*'s Print Report feature, you can do just that. Though Print Report doesn't match the elaborate report-making abilities of a high-powered database, it is still quite versatile. Choose Print Report from the File menu to see the Print Report dialog box (the figures below show the ImageWriter version.)

There are three ways to arrange report data on the page:

The Labels option prints the contents of specified fields in blocks that can be sized to be printed on standard adhesive labels. Figure 4-12 shows the Print Report box for printing labels.

Figure 4-12. Label Reports

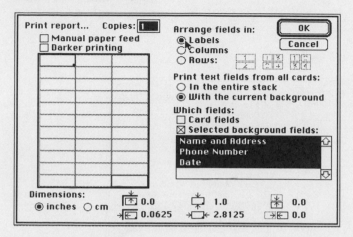

The Columns option allots a column to each field type in the typical database reporting style. Figure 4-13 shows the column version of the Print Report box. Column only works when you've checked the With the Current Background button.

Figure 4-13. Column Reports

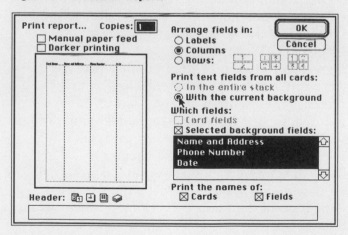

The Rows option keeps all the fields belonging to each card together in a row; this is good for printing address lists (see Figure 4-14).

Figure 4-14. Row Reports

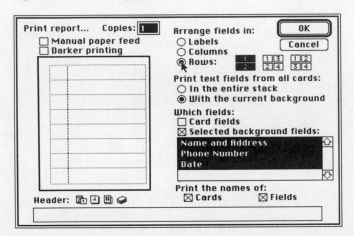

Adjust the exact spacing of rows or columns by dragging the vertical and horizontal dotted lines in the page layout window. With the Label option, dimension boxes appear at the bottom of the dialog box that let you match the exact size of the adhesive labels you plan to use.

Specifying which fields to print. You must also specify which fields you want to print. In nearly all cases, you'll be printing selected background fields from cards with the current background, that is, that have the same underlying design and layout of fields. (The difference between card fields and background fields is explained in the next chapter.)

The scrollable directory box shows you the names of all fields that meet the criteria you've specified. You can select more than one field or all the fields by clicking on them while pressing the Shift key. Unselect them by Shift-clicking on them again. Use the Field Info option in the Objects menu to find out the exact names of all the fields on the cards you plan to print.

If you're using the column or row format, it's usually helpful to print the field name along with the information it contains; this option is already checked at bottom right. Headers can be added as explained under Printing Stacks.

The Print Report options and layouts can be confusing. The best way to understand them is to try each method for yourself. The Help stacks provide good material for practice.

Protecting Stacks

You may want to limit access to the information you keep in your stacks or to prevent users from modifying a stack that you have created. Choosing the Protect Stack option in the File menu brings up the dialog box in Figure 4-15.

Figure 4-15. Protecting Stack Dialog Box

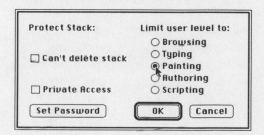

Check the Can't Modify Stack and/or Can't Delete Stack boxes if you want to make sure that others won't be able to change or remove the current stack.

Limit User Level to browsing or typing if you don't want to confuse the user with the full authoring environment, or if you want to prevent anyone from reading or modifying the scripts in your stacks. You'll still be able to get to the Protect Stack menu option by pressing the Command key and pulling down the File menu.

Check Private Access if you want to limit the use of the current stack and the Protect Stack dialog box to a user with the proper password.

Click on Set Password to tell *HyperCard* the password. In the password dialog box, you must type in the password identically twice so that its spelling can be verified. Clicking OK protects the stack. To open the stack again, you must provide the password, spelled exactly as it was in the Password dialog box. Once you've gained entry to the stack, you can change the password using the method described above.

Important: You won't be able to open the stack again without the password. *Don't forget the password.* Consider copying an important stack to another disk, and store that copy in a secure place, before password-protecting the original.

Warning: Always set the Private Access feature *before* you assign a password. If you do it the other way around, you may be locked permanently out of your stack. Also, *be sure to hit Tab, not Return, to get from the first entry of your password in the Password dialog box to the second entry.* If you hit Return instead, you may confuse the program into looking for a password that is spelled differently than the one you intended. These are bugs in *HyperCard* version 1.0.1 only; however, for maximum safety, avoid the password method of protecting your stacks and keep sensitive information on a separate disk that you can physically lock away. If your information is stored on a hard disk, use one of the commercial security utilities to create a locked area on the disk, and keep your stacks there.

Individual cards and backgrounds can be protected with options in the Card Info and Background Info dialog boxes, which are accessible through the Objects menu. You can also lock fields with the Field Info box.

At this point, you're ready to dig deeper into the structure of *HyperCard* and take on the task of creating your own cards and stacks. The next five chapters will show you how.

Chapter 5

More About Cards and Stacks

Chapter 5

More About
Cards and Stacks

Until now we've treated *HyperCard* as a terrain to be explored.
In this and the following chapters, you'll turn from passive exploration to active engineering of the *HyperCard* terrain. In the
process, you'll learn the techniques for becoming a *HyperCard*
author.

The Authoring Environment

Authoring in *HyperCard* can be defined as using the program's
tools to modify existing cards and stacks and to create your
own applications. As a *HyperCard* author, you'll be able to
take control of your computing environment in a way that you
never may have before. Rather than having to adapt to the
strictures and limitations of commercial software, you will be
able to design *HyperCard* applications that meet your own
information needs or those of your family, friends, or colleagues. Applications can be as simple as a customized file index or as complex as an interactive educational stack with
graphics, sound, and animation—the nature of your *HyperCard*
work is up to you.

This kind of freedom would not be possible if *HyperCard*
authoring were as complex and difficult to master as ordinary
Macintosh programming. In fact, *HyperCard* authoring is refreshingly simple. In large, it draws upon Macintosh editing
skills you already possess—cutting, copying, and pasting—and
on the basic understanding of *HyperCard* elements you've acquired in working with this book. To put those skills to most
effective use, however, you need to learn more about the deep
structure of *HyperCard* objects.

Objects and Properties

In *HyperCard* parlance, the main elements of the program, stacks, backgrounds, cards, fields, and buttons, are all called *objects*. An object can be worked with, modified, created, and deleted. Objects can be closely related to and can contain other objects (for example, a stack can be linked to other stacks, and a card can contain card buttons and card fields) but every object also has independent characteristics that you can determine, either by the authoring techniques described below, or by writing a script for the object as discussed in Chapters 8 and 9.

    HyperCard objects have *properties*. A *property* is any characteristic of an object, such as its name, location, or action (a button's response to a click of the mouse, for example). Properties can be *global* (they can be part of *HyperCard* itself and affect all objects in the program), or they can be very narrow, (as specific as the name of a field). Figure 5-1 lists the major *HyperCard* objects and their properties. Most authoring tasks involve setting or changing the properties of an object.

Figure 5-1. Objects and Their Properties

PROPERTY	(stack)	bkgd	(card)	(field)	◉
autoHilite					✓
hilite					✓
icon					✓
id			✓	✓	✓
location				✓	✓
lockText				✓	✓
name	✓	✓	✓	✓	✓
script	✓	✓	✓	✓	✓
scroll				✓	
showLines				✓	
showName					✓
style				✓	✓
textAlign				✓	✓
textFont				✓	✓
textHeight				✓	✓
textSize				✓	✓
textStyle				✓	✓
visible				✓	✓
wideMargins				✓	

Two special classes of properties belong to windows and the painting mode (discussed in the next chapter). *HyperCard* windows—the tear-off menus and the message box—aren't manipulable objects in the same sense that buttons or fields are, but you can specify their location. Properties of the painting mode can be set from a script; see Chapters 6, 8, and 9.

A note on name and number properties: All *HyperCard* objects can have names assigned to them. These names are not required, but are for your convenience (although it is a good idea to name any important object that you create). For example, in a stack containing a billing list, you can name one field *invoice date* and another named *invoice number*. All objects are named using their respective Info boxes, which are available from the Objects menu. An object also has a unique and permanent ID number, which is assigned to it automatically by *HyperCard*. The ID number of an object, not the name you may assign to it, enables *HyperCard* to tell that object from another similar one. Also, cards, fields, and buttons have *object numbers*, which tell you their position in relation to other similar objects. These numbers can change. For example, a card's number can change anytime you rearrange the cards in the stack, but the card's ID number will always be the same.

The Structure of Stacks and Cards

Take a look at any card. All the objects on the card appear to exist on the same plane, but, structurally, each object exists on its own *layer*. Think of each button, field, card, and background as being on its own sheet of transparent plastic. The sheets of plastic are laid one on top of the next in a very definite order to create the card you see (as in Figure 5-2). These layers are invisible to the browser, but must be carefully arranged by the *HyperCard* author.

Figure 5-2. Layers

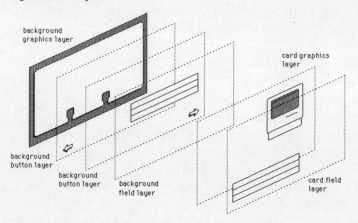

A card is composed of background layers and card layers. The background layers contain the objects and graphics common to all cards that share the same background (often, that will be all the cards in a stack). Card layers (which you can also think of as the foreground layers) contain objects and graphics specific only to one card. For example, the arrow buttons that take you forward and backward among cards in a stack will almost certainly reside on background layers; all cards in the stack have the same buttons. A field that holds information that is relevant to only one card will be on a card layer.

Every time a new object is added, a new layer is created; every time you delete an object, its layer is deleted as well. Each new layer is laid on top of existing layers. Some objects and graphics are themselves transparent, that is, they allow any lower layers to show through; and other objects and graphics are opaque, blocking the view of layers and objects directly beneath them. Therefore, thoughtful positioning and layering of objects is important. *HyperCard* provides you with the tools to rearrange the order of objects at any time with options in the Objects menu. We'll look at layer manipulation in more detail in the sections on fields and buttons in this chapter.

More on Stacks

Stacks come in two types, homogeneous and heterogeneous. Homogeneous stacks contain cards with only one background. The Addressbook and File Index are examples of homogeneous stacks: their cards all have identical backgrounds and identical functions. Heterogeneous stacks contain cards with more than one background. The Datebook, with its different backgrounds for To Do, Weekly, and Calendar, is a heterogeneous stack; it combines several different functions. The number of backgrounds you can have in a stack is limited only by the number of cards in the stack.

Information about the number of backgrounds in a stack, as well as a stack's other vital specifications, can be found in the Stack Info dialog box (see Figure 5-3) , which is always available from the Objects menu.

Figure 5-3. Stack Info Dialog Box

The File menu contains options for creating, compacting, and deleting stacks. These are analogous to the file- or document-handling options in other Macintosh programs.

To create a new stack based on a card in an existing stack:

1. Bring up the stack and card you want to use as the model. You could, for example, create a new Addressbook stack that you could customize later.
2. Select New Stack from the File menu. A dialog box will ask you to name the new stack (be sure to give it a name different from that of the stack you are using as a model) and

query whether you want to copy the current background. In this case, you do, so leave the box checked.

3. *HyperCard* will create a file for the new stack on the current disk in the folder containing the Home stack. The new stack will consist of one card with a background copied from the model card (any card objects or text in background fields will not be copied). You can then create additional cards using the background as is or customize the background and cards as described below.

Note: *HyperCard* does not automatically create a button for your new stack on the Home card. You'll have to do that yourself. The technique is described in Chapter 7.

Frequently used or modified stacks tend to get bigger and bigger, eating disk space and slowing access to information. Use the Compact Stack option to eliminate unused space in the stack; the stack will take up less room while retaining all its information. This is especially valuable for hard disk users reaching the limit of their disk's capacity (easy to do with *HyperCard*).

To compact a stack:

1. Go to the stack you want to compact.
2. Choose **Compact Stack** from the File menu.
3. The stack will compact automatically. Check the Stack Info box before and after to see the amount of unused space that has been reclaimed.

Important: *HyperCard* version 1.0.1 has a bug that affects stack compression. If you create a stack that has more than 126 background or card fields (not very likely, but not impossible), compacting the stack will result in damage to the stack. If you are using version 1.0.1, just keep the number of fields in the stack below 126. (Remember that one background field may appear on many cards, but it only needs to be counted as one field.) Large stacks containing many fields can be split into two or more stacks.

To delete a stack:

1. Go to the stack you want to delete. Try deleting the HyperCalc stack, but be sure you have a backup copy.
2. Choose **Delete Stack** from the file menu.
3. Click on Delete in the dialog box that appears. All objects in the stack will be deleted, and the stack file will be erased.
4. *HyperCard* then returns you to the Home card. Don't delete the Home stack on your *HyperCard* disks.

A note on stack names: You can change a stack's name anytime, either from the Finder or within *HyperCard* by changing the name in the Stack Info dialog box. However, if you change the name of the stack, any links to the stack from other stacks will be broken, since the links will be looking for the stack under the old name. Any links you wish to keep will have to be re-created using the new stack name. (Find out more about linking at the end of this chapter.)

More on Backgrounds

As you've learned, every card has a background. Just like cards, backgrounds can contain graphics, fields, and buttons; or they can be entirely blank. Like other objects, backgrounds can be copied and customized. Basic information on the current card's background can be obtained from the **Background Info** dialog box, available through the Objects menu (Figure 5-4).

Figure 5-4. Background Info Dialog Box

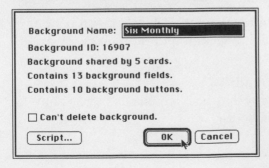

You can prevent a user from unintentionally modifying or deleting the background by clicking on the Can't Modify Background and Can't Delete Background check boxes.

To see or work with a background, you must be in background mode. To see what background mode is like, go to one of the Calendar cards and choose Background from the Edit menu, or type Command-B. (The Background menu option will get a check mark.) Figure 5-5 shows the differences between normal mode and background mode. You can always tell when you are in background mode by the striped border on the menu bar. To exit background mode, choose Background from the Edit menu again, or type Command-B again.

Note that only the background's graphics, fields, and buttons are visible in background mode. Text in background fields, as well as objects or graphics in any card layers, are invisible. Sometimes, details may appear that you can't see in normal mode because they were obscured by opaque graphics or objects in card layers above them.

The techniques for customizing backgrounds (adding and deleting fields, buttons, and graphics) are essentially the same as those for customizing cards, which are discussed in the sections on cards, fields, and buttons below.

To copy a background:

1. Copy a card with that background.
2. Delete any card objects.

To create a new background:

1. Choose **New Background** from the Objects menu.
2. *HyperCard* creates a blank background on a blank card, ready for customizing.

To delete a background:
Delete every card with that background. If there is only one card in the stack, delete the stack.

Figure 5-5. Normal Mode vs. Background Mode

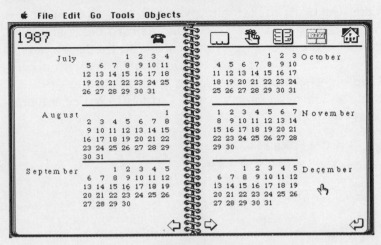

Background mode

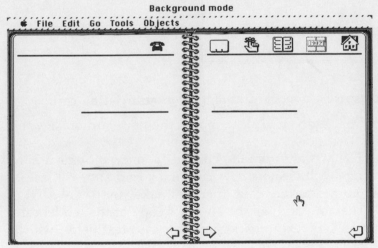

More on Cards

A card consists of its background, which it may share with
other cards in a stack; any objects, such as card fields and card
buttons, that are unique to that one card; and the text in any
fields on the card, including background fields. As with other
HyperCard objects, you can get information about the current
card from the Objects menu. Choose **Card Info** to see the dialog box in Figure 5-6.

Figure 5-6. Card Info Dialog Box

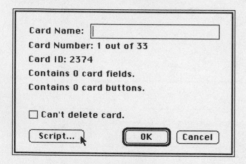

Card Name:
Card Number: 1 out of 33
Card ID: 2374
Contains 0 card fields.
Contains 0 card buttons.

☐ Can't delete card.

[Script...]   (OK)   [Cancel]

To create a new card modeled on an existing card:

1. Go to the card you want to model the new card on. Try this
   with a File Index card.
2. Choose **New Card** from the Edit menu, or type Command-N.
3. *HyperCard* will create a new File Index card and will insert
   it behind the current card, then will take you to the new
   card. The new card will be an exact copy of the model card,
   except for any text in background or card text fields, which
   will not be transferred.

To delete a card:

1. Go to the card you want to cut. You can cut the File Index
   card you just created.
2. Choose **Cut Card** from the Edit menu, or type Command-X.
   HyperCard cuts the card from the stack, saves it to the Clipboard (erasing anything that might already be in the Clipboard), and puts up the next card.

Alternatively, you can:

Choose **Delete** from the Edit menu. This deletes the card and all its objects completely and permanently. *HyperCard* takes you to the next card.

To move a card to another position in the same stack:

1. Go to the card you want to move. (You might try moving a card in the Weekly part of the Datebook.)
2. Choose **Cut Card** from the Edit menu, or type Command-X. *HyperCard* deletes the card from the stack, saves it to the Clipboard (erasing anything that might already be in the Clipboard), and puts up the next card.
3. Go to the card just before the place you want to insert the cut card.
4. Insert the card using **Paste** in the Edit menu, or type Command-V. *HyperCard* will paste the card, with its background and all associated objects (including the text in text fields), after the current card; and then it will take you to the inserted card. Open Card Info before and after moving the card to see how the card's card number has changed.

To copy a card to another stack:

1. Go to the card you want to copy. We'll copy an Addressbook card to the Datebook, so go to the first card of that stack.
2. Choose **Copy** from the Edit menu, or type Command-C. *HyperCard* copies the entire card to the Clipboard (erasing anything that might already be there).
3. Go to the Datebook, then go to the card before the place you want to insert the card copy (in this case, we'll make it the last card in the To Do list).
4. Insert the card using **Paste** in the Edit menu, or type Command-V. *HyperCard* will paste the card, with its background and all associated objects (including the text in text fields), after the current card; and then it will take you to the inserted card.
5. The stack will gain a new background (the background of the Addressbook card), as you'll see if you check the Stack Info dialog box.

More on Fields

In this section, we'll work with a card in the Quotations stack in the *HyperCard* stacks folder, so go to Quotations now.

Fields hold most of the information you'll be storing in *HyperCard* (graphics contain the rest). There can be as many fields on a card as will reasonably fit; fields can even be overlapped and hidden. To do any work with fields (beyond simply entering text into them), you must activate the field tool in the Tools menu. When the field tool is on, you can see the outlines of all the fields on the card, whether they are background or card fields. Select the left-hand field by clicking on it; its outline will turn into a marquee (as in Figure 5-7).

Figure 5-7. Selected Field

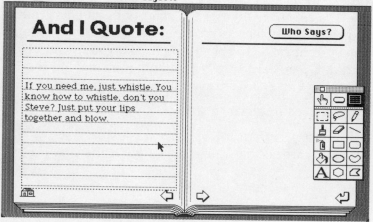

Note that the phrase *And I Quote:* is not outlined. That's because it is not text in a field. *And I Quote:* is *graphic text* in the card's background graphics layer. Graphic text is created with *HyperCard*'s graphic tools and is not typed into a text field. Graphic text cannot be edited like field text; it can only be created, altered, or removed with the graphics tools. (We'll examine *HyperCard* graphics in the next chapter.) You may find it easier to think of graphic text as *inert* and field text as *active.* It's important to keep the distinction between field text and graphic text in mind when you begin to design your own cards and stacks.

Fields have many more properties than stacks, backgrounds, or cards, as you'll see if you look at the Field Info dialog box (Figure 5-8). You can also see the Field Info box by double-clicking on the selected field. If you're not in field mode, you can still see the Field Info box by moving the *I*-beam text cursor to the field and choosing Field Info.

Figure 5-8. Field Info Dialog Box

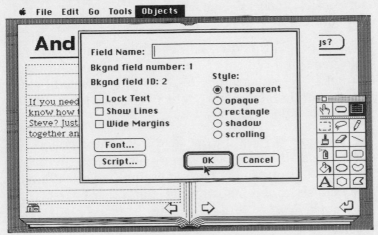

As you can see from the box, the selected field is a background field; it's shared by all the cards in the stack. Most fields you'll encounter and create will be background fields, but not all. Card fields, though rarer, also have their uses. For example, imagine you're creating a *HyperCard* catalogue of hand tools, including pictures in various sizes. You want to include a caption below a picture of a set of wood gouges describing the gouges' fine boxwood handles. Only a card field will do for the caption, since other cards in the stack would not need that field in that location.

Note that the field has no name. You can give it a name by entering *Quote* into the Field Name: section of the dialog box. Though names are not especially important for backgrounds or cards, they are for fields, and you should get into the habit of naming every field you create.

There is one practical aspect of field names and numbers that you can put to use immediately. You can limit text searches to specific fields if you know the number or name of the field. Use this format in the message box:

find "[search word]" in field [number] [name]

For example:

find "janet" in field company contact
find "fossil" in field 12

The field's other properties are set with buttons in the rest of the dialog box. You can choose among five styles and three formats of field. Try out each of these with the selected field, toggling between the browse and field tool to see what effect each option has.

• Lock text prevents any text in the field from being edited.
• Transparent fields let any object or graphics below the field show through. Opaque fields hide anything underneath. All the other field styles, no matter what their other characteristics, are opaque.
• A scrolling field lets you put more text into a field than fits on the screen—in fact, you can type up to 32K of text, about 16 pages, into a scrolling field. Use the scroll bar to read to the bottom of the field.

The font, style, alignment, and line height of the text in the field can be changed. Click on the **Font** button in the Field Info box to see your choices from the Text Style dialog box (Figure 5-9). Try several different fonts, styles, and line heights to get a feel for the possibilities. You can double-click on a font or font size to select it and close the Text Style dialog box at the same time. The Text Style dialog box is also available through the Edit menu; select a field and then choose Text Style.

Figure 5-9. Text Style Dialog Box

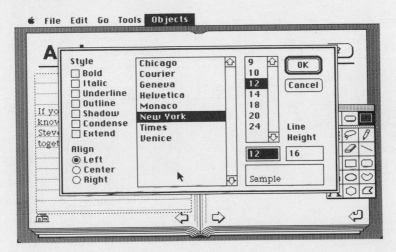

Keep in mind that the fonts shown are the ones that are installed in the System file on your *HyperCard* disk. Not everyone will have the same fonts on their Macintosh. Text in a different font may not fit properly into a carefully sized field. If you're designing stacks for others, it's safest to specify field text in one of the System fonts, Geneva 9 and 12, Monaco 9, and Chicago 12, that are permanently installed in every System.

There is a hidden field on this card. Reactivate the browse tool and click on the Who Says button to see it (Figure 5-10). We'll use this field for practicing field manipulation.

Figure 5-10. The Hidden Field

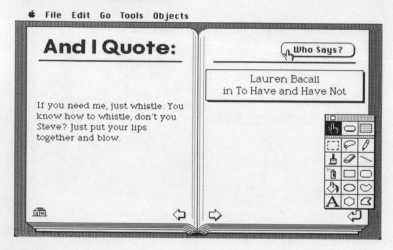

To move a field:

1. Activate the field tool.
2. Position the pointer over the center of the field.
3. Drag the field to a new location anywhere on the card. You can move the field over another field. If the field is a background field, which this one is, every card that shares the background will be affected. Check another card in the stack to see.

To change the size of a field:

1. Activate the field tool.
2. Position the pointer over one of the field's corners.
3. Drag the corner to resize the field. The opposite corner remains stationary.
4. Text in the field will wrap to fit the new field dimensions. If you make the field too small to display all the text, the last part of the text will be cut off, but it remains part of the field and will reappear if you make the field larger again.
5. Again, if the field is a background field, every card that shares the background will be affected.

To create a field:

1. Activate the field tool.
2. Decide if you want a card or background field. In this case, you'll make a background field, so enter background mode by choosing Background from the Edit menu or pressing Command-B.
3. Choose **New Field** from the Objects menu. A new, empty field will appear in the center of the screen. Drag it to the bottom of the right-hand page.
4. Make style and format choices via the Field Info and Fonts dialog boxes.
5. Size the field and test it with some text. The created field is shown in Figure 5-11.

Figure 5-11. New Field

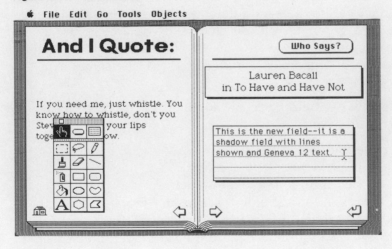

To delete a field:

1. Activate the field tool.
2. Select the field (pick the one you just created).
3. Choose **Cut Field** from the Edit menu, or press Command-X. The field is saved to the Clipboard.

Alternatively, you can

1. Choose **Clear Field** to completely delete the field.
2. If the field is a background field, you will delete it from all cards sharing the background.

To clone a field on the same card:

1. Activate the field tool.
2. Select the field you want to clone.
3. Put the pointer over the field, press the Option key, and drag the pointer to the location where you want the new field.
4. A duplicate of the field will peel off and follow the pointer to the new location. This duplicates the field only, not any text that may be in the field.
5. Open the Field Info dialog box to check the stats of the new field. Note that it has a different and higher number than the field from which it was cloned. If you are cloning a background field, the new field will be a background field also, and it will appear on all cards with the same background.

To move a field back and forth from the card to the background layer:

1. Activate the field tool.
2. Select the field you want to move.
3. Check Field Info to see what domain (card or background) the field is in, or just enter background mode to see if the field is still there. If it is, it's a background field.
4. To move a background field to the card layer, enter background mode, cut the field, exit background mode, and paste the field on the card.
5. To move a card field to the background, cut the field, enter background mode, and paste the field to the background.
6. Check Field Info to confirm.

To copy a field to another card:

1. Activate the field tool.
2. Select the field you want to copy.
3. Copy it to the Clipboard.
4. Go to the stack and card you want to copy the field to.
5. Choose **Paste** form the Edit menu (or Command-V). The field will appear on the screen. Move and size the field as needed. If it is a background field, it will appear on all cards that share the field.
6. This process only copies the field, not any text that may be in the field. You must perform an extra step if you want to copy the text as well. To copy text, select, copy, and paste it like any other Macintosh text.

As you'll recall, when you're entering text on a card with several fields, you can jump from one field to the next by hitting the Tab key. Actually, when you hit Tab, *HyperCard* takes you to the field layer one step closer to the top level, working from background fields to card fields. Another way of saying this is that *HyperCard* tabs you from the first field that was created for the card (which occupies the bottom field layer, and has the lowest field number) to the field most recently created (the top field layer, with the highest field number). Figure 5-12 shows how this works.

Figure 5-12. Field Layer Order

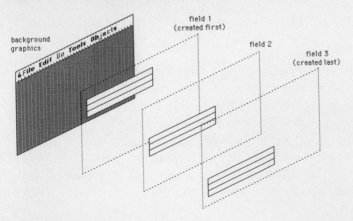

When you're creating or customizing a card with several fields, you need to keep the order of the fields in mind. Luckily, *HyperCard* provides you with tools for moving fields (and buttons) to put them into any order required. These are the **Bring Closer** (Command-+) and **Send Farther** (Command- −) options in the Objects menu. These will move a selected field up or down one layer at a time. For example, moving field 3 in Figure 5-12 two steps back results in the order shown in Figure 5-13.

Figure 5-13. Field Layer 2

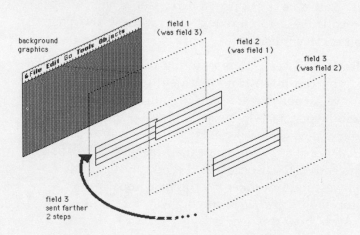

In chapter 7, you'll be working more with field layer order.

More on Buttons

In this section, we'll be working with buttons on the File Index, Addressbook, and Home cards, so make sure these are available. Go to the first card in the File Index now.

So far you've used buttons mainly as a kind of rapid transit system, speeding you from one part of *HyperCard* to the next. If you've worked through the *HyperCard* Intro and the Help stacks, you've also seen that buttons are smart switches that can initiate any *HyperCard* action.

Like fields, buttons have many properties and can be manipulated with great flexibility. They come in a multitude of styles, can take on a very wide range of visual attributes, and can be programmed to perform any task.

All authoring work with buttons must be done in button mode, with the button tool activated. Tear off the Tools menu and select the button tool. You'll see boxes around all the buttons, showing you their actual sizes and proportions (buttons are always rectangular). Select the **New** button and choose **Button Info** from the Objects menu, or just double-click on the button. You'll be presented with the Button Info dialog box (Figure 5-14).

Figure 5-14. Button Info Dialog Box

Use this box to learn about and modify the properties of the selected button.

* Buttons have names, numbers, and IDs just like fields. The button's number depends on its layer order.
* **Show Name** lets you toggle the button's name on and off. Try it with the New button. You can also do this with other buttons like the Next button (the right arrow), but you won't be able to see the button's name unless you make the button larger (see below for how to do that).

• Check **Auto hilite** to make the button show reverse black-and-white when you click on it.

There are seven button styles. Most of them will be familiar to you already.

• Transparent buttons show any graphics or objects underneath.
• Opaque buttons hide anything underneath them.
• Check box and radio buttons are good to use when an option can be toggled on and off, or when you are presenting a list of choices and you want to provide feedback to the user about what choice has been made.

The **Icon** button takes you to the Icon Selection dialog box shown in Figure 5-15. A button icon is a picture attached to a button—the icon is a property of the button and goes with the button wherever the button goes. By contrast, many buttons do not have icons; for example most of the buttons on the Home card are simply transparent buttons placed over graphics. These graphics have no connection to the buttons (beyond appearing to be in the same place on the card) and will stay on the card even if the buttons are moved or deleted.

Figure 5-15. Button Icons

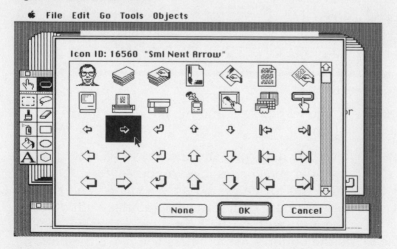

Only an icon shown in the Icon dialog box can be attached to a button. Assign an icon to the selected button, or change an existing icon, by clicking on the desired icon and then choosing OK. Remove an icon from a button by clicking on None.

With the various styles and icons available, you have nearly unlimited ways to vary the appearance of buttons. Try a few choices on the New button for yourself.

Link To enables you to create a simple link or path to any card or stack.

To use Link To:

1. Activate the button tool.
2. Double-click on the button that will carry the link. For this exercise, we'll use the Home button at lower left.
3. Click on the **Link** button. You'll see the Link To dialog box (Figure 5-16).

Figure 5-16. Link to Dialog Box

4. Go to the card or stack you want to link. Let's make a link to the first card of the Addressbook, so go to that card now. The Link To dialog box remains on the screen.
5. Click **This Card** if you want a link to the current card, or **This Stack** if you want a link to the first card in the current stack. In this case, either will do.
6. *HyperCard* will forge the link and return you to your starting point (in this case, the File Index card).
7. Try the new link to see if it works. Instead of going to Home, the Home button should now take you to the first card of the Addressbook.
8. Select a new icon for the button to finish the job.

Not all buttons can be relinked in this way—it depends on what other tasks the button is performing at the same time. New links are best made with new buttons.

The techniques for moving, copying, creating, and deleting buttons follow the same principles described for manipulating fields. You can use the File Index's New button for the following.

To move a button:

1. Activate the button tool.
2. Position the pointer over the center of the button you want to move.
3. Drag the button to a new location anywhere on the card. If the button is a background button, which this one is, every card that shares the background will be affected. Check another card in the stack to see.

To change the size of a button:

1. Activate the button tool.
2. Position the pointer over one of the button's corners.
3. Drag the corner to resize the button. The opposite corner remains stationary.
4. A name in the button will wrap to fit the new button dimensions. If you make the button too small to display all the name, some part of the name will be cut off, but it remains part of the button and will reappear if you make the button larger again.
5. Again, if the button is a background button, every card that shares the background will be affected.

To create a button:

1. Activate the button tool.
2. Decide if you want a card or background button. In this case, you'll make a background button, so enter background mode by choosing Background from the Edit menu or by pressing Command-B.
3. Choose **New Button** from the Objects menu. A new, empty button will appear in the center of the screen. Drag it to the bottom of the right-hand page.

4. Make style and format choices via the **Button Info** and Icon dialog boxes. Create a link for the button with the **Link To** option.

To delete a button:

1. Activate the button tool.
2. Select the button (pick the one you just created).
3. Choose **Cut Button** from the Edit menu, or press Command-X. The button is saved to the Clipboard.

Alternatively, you can:

1. Choose **Clear Button** to completely delete the button.
2. If the button is a background button, you will delete it from all cards sharing the background.

To clone a button on the same card:

1. Activate the button tool.
2. Select the button you want to clone.
3. Put the pointer over the button, press the Option key, and drag the pointer to the location where you want the new button.
4. A duplicate of the button will peel off and follow the pointer to the new location. This duplicates the entire button, including any links or other actions the button may perform.
5. Open the Button Info dialog box to check the properties of the new button. Note that it has a different and higher number than the button from which it was cloned. If you are cloning a background button, the new button will be a background button also, and it will appear on all cards with the same background.

To move a button back and forth between the card and the background layer:

1. Activate the button tool.
2. Select the button you want to move.
3. Check **Button Info** to see what domain (card or background) the button is in, or just enter background mode to see if the button is still there. If it is, it's a background button.

4. To move a background button to the card layer, enter background mode, cut the button, exit background mode, and paste the button on the card.
5. To move a card button to the background, cut the button, enter background mode, and paste the button to the background.
6. Check **Button Info** to confirm.

To copy a button to another card:

1. Activate the button tool.
2. Select the button you want to copy.
3. Copy it to the Clipboard.
4. Go to the stack and card you want to copy the button to.
5. Choose Paste (or Command-V). The button will appear on the screen.

Move and size the button as needed. If it is a background button, it will appear on all cards that share the button.

To overlap buttons:

1. Activate the button tool.
2. Move a small button over a large one. The small button will block the action of the larger button only in the area that the smaller button occupies. Make sure that there is enough area left to click on the larger button.
3. Test the results. Each button will retain its individual function.
4. If you move a large button completely over a smaller button, the large button will completely block the action of the smaller one.

One area of authoring that we haven't touched on yet is *HyperCard* graphics. That's the subject of the next chapter.

Chapter 6
HyperCard Graphics

Chapter 6
HyperCard Graphics

HyperCard provides you with full-featured graphics tools built right into the program to help you customize the look of your cards and stacks. In this chapter, we'll review the use of these tools and will learn how to apply them to your own authoring projects.

Creating Art with *HyperCard*

You may be wondering why you should incorporate graphics into your *HyperCard* stacks at all. The answer is, of course, that you don't have to. An unlimited number of completely functional stacks can be created just with fields and buttons. Many other stacks, however, will depend on graphics—picture databases, point-of-sale stacks, and most educational stacks, to name a few examples. You'll often find that a picture can be easier for the stack user to understand and work with than any number of words or numerals—that, after all, is the philosophy behind the Macintosh's user interface. With *HyperCard*'s graphic tools, you can create whatever pictures you need and at the same time give your stacks an individuality that marks them immediately as yours.

If you're a new Macintosh owner, chances are you've never used a computer to create art. Relax, because *HyperCard* art is both undemanding and easy to learn. You use computer analogs to familiar tools, like pencils, brushes, and spray cans, and you work on an electronic canvas. While no computer program can turn you into a great artist or designer, you'll find that many mundane design tasks are far easier on the Macintosh than on paper; the computer does most of the hard work, such as drawing straight lines and perfectly proportioned shapes, copying and moving parts of pictures, and instantly erasing anything you don't like. You can concentrate on the important things, like creating a clear design that communicates just what you want to say. And if you have little artistic skill, there is a wealth of readymade art supplied with *HyperCard* and available commercially that you can adapt for your own use.

If you are an experienced Macintosh user, you are probably an expert with other Macintosh paint programs, such as *MacPaint* and *FullPaint*. *HyperCard*'s graphics tools are based on *MacPaint* concepts and tools (Bill Atkinson, the creator of *HyperCard*, also wrote *MacPaint*), so you'll have no trouble learning them. *HyperCard* has many additional graphics features, however, that are detailed below.

Like *MacPaint, HyperCard* is a *bitmap editor*; that is, you paint dot by dot on the screen, turning each screen dot (called a *pixel*) black or white to create a picture. You can use the entire screen area (which is 512 pixels wide by 342 pixels high) or any part of it as your canvas. You cannot create pictures larger than the screen, nor can you work in more than one window at a time, and *HyperCard* does not support color graphics for the Macintosh II.

Graphics Layers

Graphics have their own layers, just like objects. A graphic can be in the background or card layer, but, within the background or card domains, graphics are always behind fields and buttons. Card graphics overlaid on a background field obscure text entered into the field, but background buttons can work right through card graphics, even if you can't see the button. Figure 6-1 illustrates graphics layering.

Typically, a stack author will first design the background graphics for the cards in the stack. Background graphics are likely to contain a border (perhaps one that looks like a notebook page or an index card) and a title for the stack. Background fields and buttons will be fitted into this basic design. Then, each card may have graphics layers of its own that overlay parts of the background graphic. You cannot move graphics in front of objects in the same domain—you cannot obscure a card button with a card graphic.

Figure 6-1. Graphics Layers

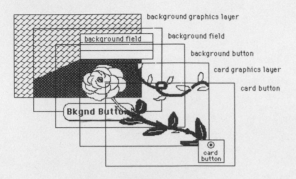

The Painting Tools

The best way to introduce yourself to the graphics tools is to experiment with them. First, create a new stack with a new background and name it *Paint Tests*. Tear off the **Tools** menu and position it at the left side of the screen. In *HyperCard* parlance, it now becomes a *palette*. Note that you can move the Tools palette anywhere on the screen using the drag bar at its top, and that you can close the palette with a close box at its upper left. Even after you've torn off a Tools palette, it is still available from the menu bar, but you can't tear off two Tools palettes at the same time—try it and see what happens.

Contained in the Tools menu are the basic graphics tools for drawing, painting, erasing, shape creation, and creating graphic text. The tools are labeled in Figure 6-2.

Figure 6-2. Labeled Tools Menu

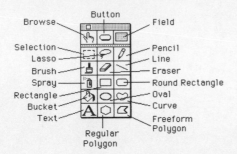

Select the tool that looks like a pencil (it's called, appropriately enough, the *Pencil*) by clicking on it. Immediately you'll see three new menus—Paint, Options, and Patterns—appear in the menu bar. (The Objects menu reappears when you choose a general tool again.) Pull the new menus down to take a look at them.

The Paint menu provides commands for changing selected parts of your picture. Figure 6-3 shows the Paint menu.

Figure 6-3. The Paint Menu

The Options menu contains drawing and painting aids and lets you choose among options for certain tools. It's illustrated in Figure 6-4.

Figure 6-4. The Options Menu

The Patterns menu consists of standard patterns that you can paint with and use to fill any shape. You can select any pattern by clicking on it. Patterns is a tear-off menu and, like Tools, can be placed anywhere on the screen. The Patterns menu is shown in Figure 6-5.

Figure 6-5. The Patterns Menu

A few tools and most graphics menu options can be operated directly from the keyboard using *power keys*. The most
important power keys are included in the following description of the graphics tools. A complete list of all graphics keyboard shortcuts can be found in Appendix B.

Pencil

Since you have the Pencil activated, let's try out that tool first.
Move to the center of the screen, where the pointer turns into
a pencil. Drag the Pencil, and a one-pixel-wide black line follows. Without letting up on the mouse button, scribble a bit or
try a simple line drawing to get a feel for how the pencil re-
sponds. When you're done with a line and want to start drawing in another spot, let up on the mouse, move the Pencil, and
start dragging again. If you start dragging when the Pencil is
over a black area, you'll leave a white line instead of a black
one.

Undo and Erase

Suppose you don't like what you've just drawn. *HyperCard* offers two ways to remedy that. Select **Undo,** an option from the
Edit menu, or press ~ (tilde) to undo your last mouse action. It
vanishes without a trace. Now, suppose you've changed your
mind and you want that part of your drawing back. Choose
Undo again, and it will reappear—Undo undoes itself.

You can also erase painlessly. Select the **Erase** tool and
move out to the drawing area. The pointer becomes a square
that you can drag over any part of your picture to erase that
area—try it now. You can clear the entire screen, erasing
everything you've drawn, by double-clicking on the Erase tool.
Use Undo to recover from any erasing that goes too far.

Selection and Lasso

With these tools, you can isolate and manipulate parts of your
picture without affecting other parts. To see what the **Selection** tool can do, draw a new picture or restore your old one to
the screen. Now choose Selection (see Figure 6-2). Draw a selection box around any part of the picture by dragging a box
over it with the crosshairs. The selected area will be outlined
in the familiar marquee or crawling dots. Once the area is se-

lected, you can move it to any other part of the screen by putting the pointer in the center of the selection and dragging it; operate on it with the Edit functions; Cut, Copy Paste, and Clear; or manipulate it further with the Paint menu.

The **Lasso** tool works similarly, but it doesn't select a rectangular area. Instead, you use the Lasso to draw a loop around the area you want to select. This tool is handy for selecting irregular shapes or for selecting small regions in tight spaces.

Try selecting parts of your picture with both tools and then cutting and pasting the parts in different areas of the screen. An easy way to make a quick copy of your selection is to press the Option key just before you start to drag the selection (this works just like copying buttons and fields, which you tried in the last chapter). If you want to constrain the movement of the selected area to the horizontal or vertical only (good for lining up several copies of the selection), press Shift before you start to drag. Note that the most recently selected area stays selected until you choose another tool or select a new area. To select everything on the screen, double-click on the Selection tool. Figure 6-6 demonstrates the uses of Selection and Lasso.

Figure 6-6. Using Selection and Lasso

Brush

Use the Brush to draw with different shapes. Select among 32 different brushes with the Brush Shape dialog box, which you can call up by double-clicking on the Brush tool. The box is shown in Figure 6-7.

Figure 6-7. Brush Shape Dialog Box

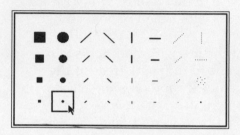

Click on any of the brush shapes to select it; the dialog box then disappears. You'll find that the diagonal brushes are good for calligraphic effects, the dotted brushes for stippling and drawing more than one line at a time. All of the brushes will paint in the current pattern—try a few patterns to see how this works. See Figure 6-8 for an illustration of the Brush in action.

Spray

Spray works somewhat like an artist's airbrush or a can of spray paint. Unlike the dotted brushes, Spray only draws dots, not lines. You drag it back and forth over an area to create a shaded or clouded area in the current pattern. Add quick clicks of Spray to create textures or stippled areas. Spray also paints in the current pattern. Spray is shown in Figure 6-8.

Bucket

Any closed shape you draw can be filled with the current pattern by using the Bucket. Just place the tip of the Bucket's drip within the area you want to fill and click. Be sure that the shape is completely bounded—any gaps in the shape will allow the pattern to spill out into the rest of the painting. If that happens, use Undo, then close any gaps you find in the shape with the Pencil or the Brush. The Bucket is also shown in Figure 6-8.

Figure 6-8. Brush, Spray, and Fill

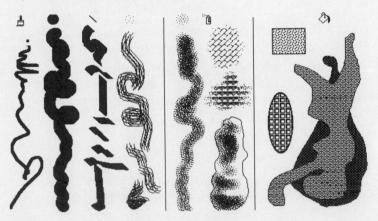

Line
The Line tool, reasonably enough, draws straight lines. Select the Line tool, click where you want the line to begin, then drag to the endpoint—a perfectly straight line will be drawn between.

Double-click on the Line tool to bring up the Line Size dialog box (Figure 6-9). Choose from any of the six line weights, or use the power keys 1, 2, 3, 4, 5 or 6, 7 or 8, with 1 being the thinnest line and 8 the thickest. The use of the Line tool is shown in Figure 6-10.

Rectangle and Rounded Rectangle
These shape tools enable you to make instant boxes and squares in any proportions. The only functional difference between them is that the rounded rectangle has rounded corners, which some people find aesthetically more pleasing.

To use either tool, set the pointer where you want one corner of the box and drag to the opposite corner. The rectangle will be drawn in the current line size. To draw a rectangle outlined in the current pattern, press the Option key just

Figure 6-9. Line Size Dialog Box

before you drag. To draw a rectangle filled in the current pattern, double-click on the tool icon—it will turn into a *filled* icon. Double-click again to return to drawing outlines. To draw a filled rectangle with no border, press the Option key just before you drag. To make squares with either tool, press the Shift key just before you drag. Figure 6-10 shows the rectangle tools.

Oval

The oval tool makes ellipses that you can size along the horizontal or vertical dimensions (you can't tilt ovals at an oblique angle). The various pattern and border variations described above for the rectangle tools apply to ovals, too (see Figure 6-10). To make circles, press Shift just before you drag.

Curve

Draw irregular curves with the Curve tool. Like the other shape tools, you can draw and fill with any line size and pattern (see Figure 6-10).

Figure 6-10. Line and Shape Tools

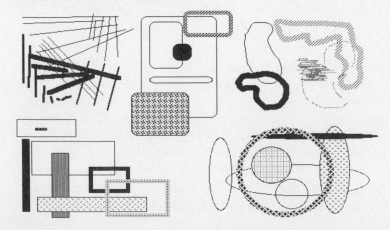

Regular Polygons

With this tool you can draw any of six shapes with equal sides—equilateral triangles, squares, pentagons, hexagons, octagons, and circles (which you can think of as polygons with an infinite number of equal sides). Choose the polygon you want to draw from the Polygon Sides dialog box (Figure 6-11), accessible by double-clicking on the Regular Polygon tool.

Figure 6-11. Polygon Sides Dialog Box

Regular polygons are created from the center out—drag until you reach the diameter you want. If you continue to hold down the mouse button, you can also rotate the polygon around its center by moving the pointer in a circle. Filled and bordered regular polygons are obtained in the same ways as with the other shape tools. Some regular polygons are shown in Figure 6-12.

Freeform Polygon

This creates polygons with any number and length of legs (sides); see Figure 6-12. Simply click once at every vertex (where a new leg of the polygon begins), and the line will follow. Double-click to finish the form. Connect the first and last legs of the polygon to complete the form yourself, or just double-click the mouse to let *HyperCard* draw the last leg for you. Freeform polygons can be filled and bordered as above.

Figure 6-12. Polygons

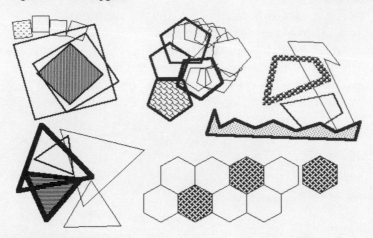

Graphic Text

Add text to your art with this tool. When you choose the text tool, the pointer becomes an *I*-beam cursor that you can position anywhere on screen and type within the current font and style. You have access to all the same fonts and styles that you do with field text; double-click on the text tool to bring up the Text Style dialog box (Figure 5-10) to see you choices. Remember that graphic text cannot be edited like field text once you choose a new tool or exit painting mode—you can only paint over it to make changes.

Graphic text is laid down as black letters on an opaque white background block. Choose **Invert** from the Paint menu after typing to turn the text into white letters on a black ground; choose **Transparent** from the Paint menu after typing to let a pattern show through around the letters (as in Figure 6-13). See more on Invert and Transparent below.

When the Graphic Text tool is activated, the power keys are temporarily disabled.

Figure 6-13. Graphic Text

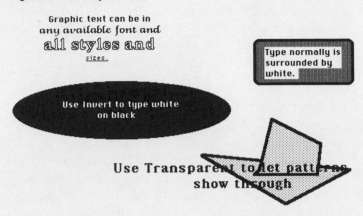

The Paint Menu

The Paint menu contains the following options.

Select (power key S)
This selects the last object drawn

Select All (power key A)
This selects the whole screen; it is equivalent to double-clicking the Selection tool.

Fill (power key F)
This fills the selected area or the last-drawn shape with the current pattern. Fill works like the Bucket tool.

Invert (power key I)
Invert turns black pixels white and white pixels black in the selected area, yielding a negative image. Toggle Invert on and off (by pressing the I key) to see whether the selected area looks better inverted or in its original values. Take a look at Figure 6-14 for an example of Invert.

Pickup (power key P)

This lets you select an image using the outline of a shape tool. First, cover the image you wish to pick up with a filled borderless shape—say, a circle. Then choose Pickup. The area within the circle will be selected, ready for more manipulations (as in Figure 6-14).

Darken (power key D) and Lighten (power key L)

These options randomly add black or white pixels to the selected or last-drawn area (see Figure 6-14). Use them to change an area's value, to make an area less well-defined (like a mountain seen in the distance), or to create random textures.

Darken and Lighten can be invoked repeatedly for additive effects; ultimately you can get an entirely black or an entirely white area.

Trace Edges (power key E)

This will outline the selected or most recently painted shape. It adds a one-pixel border completely surrounding any mark or shape, while turning the mark or shape white. Trace Edges can be done repeatedly by just holding down the E key (see Figure 6-14).

Figure 6-14. Invert, Pickup, Darken, Lighten, Trace Edges

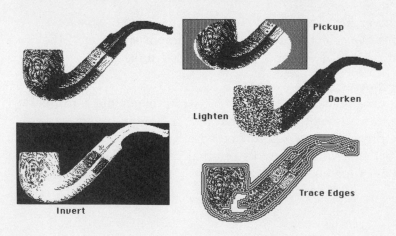

Rotate Left (power key [) and Rotate Right (power key])
These commands rotate the selected area of last object drawn in 90-degree increments, either clockwise (right) or counterclockwise (left) around the selection's center. See Figure 6.15 for examples of rotated graphics.

You'll find that *HyperCard* will try to prevent you from rotating an object so that some part of it goes off the screen by moving the entire object away from the edge. If you do manage to rotate an object partly off the screen (for example, if you try to rotate an object that is as wide as the screen), you'll lose the part that went offscreen.

Flip Vertical (power key V) and Flip Horizontal (power key H)
Use the Flip commands to create mirror images of the selected or most recently drawn object. Flip Vertical creates a mirror image reflected along a horizontal line; Flip Horizontal creates a mirror image reflected along a vertical line (see Figure 6-15). Flipping is most useful for creating bilaterally symmetrical objects like vases, buildings, reflections, and so on.

Opaque (power key O) and Transparent (power key T)
Opaque makes the selected or most recently drawn area completely opaque, even any white parts that may have been transparent. Transparent makes all white areas in the selection clear, so that anything behind the selection will show through. These options are demonstrated in Figure 6-15.

You can get a better idea of how Opaque and Transparent work by creating two rectangles filled with the same pattern. Select one rectangle, choose Opaque, then pass it over the second. Now choose Transparent and pass the selected rectangle over the other one again. Notice how the pattern changes in the top rectangle as it passes over the other. Interesting intersecting patterns can be created in this way.

Typing Option-O will show you all the areas on the screen that are opaque by making them black while you press the keys. This is quite useful because, at a glance, you can't tell opaque white from transparent white.

Figure 6-15. Rotating, Flipping, Opaque, and Transparent

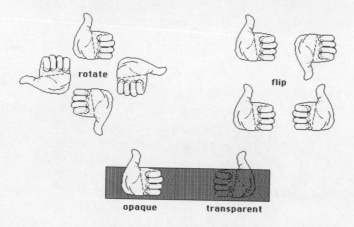

Keep (power key K) and Revert (power key R)

While you are painting, *HyperCard* suspends its usual practice of automatically saving your work every few minutes. This allows you to experiment with an existing picture without worrying that you'll save over it and possibly ruin it. Keep allows you to decide when you want to save your work—just choose it when you are satisfied with what you've painted.

It is not really necessary to use Keep to save your graphic work if you're just making a minor change. *HyperCard* will save what you've done when you exit the painting mode or when you leave the stack or program. But for extended painting, regular Keeping is important.

If you don't like the way your painting looks but you've gone too far to simply Undo the problem, you can return to the last saved version of your painting with the Revert command.

The Options Menu

The Options menu gives you access to additional tools that affect all painting operations.

Grid (power key G)

The Grid imposes an invisible, 8 X 8 pixel grid on the screen. The grid constrains certain tools—the selection, line, rectangle, rounded rectangle, oval, and polygon tools—so that they operate only along the grid lines or center on its vertices. This makes precise spacing and alignment of graphic elements easy to achieve—a boon for all kinds of design work.

A good way to see how the Grid works is to make it visible (as in Figure 6-16). Here's how:

To make the Grid visible:

1. Turn on the Grid.
2. Select the Line tool.
3. Draw a few parallel horizontal lines with the closest possible spacing (8 pixels). Now draw a few vertical parallel lines intersecting the horizontal lines.
4. Select the intersecting lines.
5. Paint the entire screen with them using the Copy function or by pressing the Option key and peeling off additional copies.
6. Now try the other painting tools to see the Grid's effects more clearly.

Figure 6-16. Visible Grid

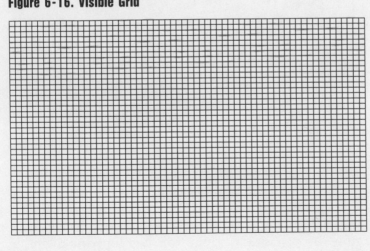

FatBits (Option-F)

FatBits is *HyperCard*'s magnifying glass for doing detail work. The best way to understand this is to try it. Enter FatBits by choosing it from the Options menu, by double-clicking on the Pencil, by pressing Option-F, or by positioning the Pencil on the screen, pressing the Command key, and clicking. You'll see a section of your drawing (64 × 43 pixels) in high magnification, as in Figure 6-17. All the painting tools work in Fatbits, so you can make small, exact alterations to your painting that would be hard to do at the normal 72 pixel-per-inch scale.

A small window opens that shows you the magnified area in normal scale. You can move and close this window just as you do with the palettes.

Figure 6-17. FatBits

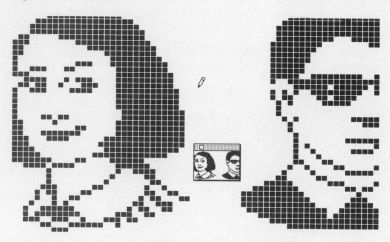

Scroll around the screen while in FatBits by pressing the Option key. A hand appears in place of the pointer; drag the hand to pull or push the view until you see the part you want. Let up on the Option key to return to the tool you were using.

Exit FatBits by choosing it again from the Options menu (it will lose its check mark), by double-clicking on the Pencil again, by pressing Option-F again, by pressing Command and clicking with the Pencil, or by clicking in the small window.

Power Keys

This toggles on and off the ability to use the power keys. You can ensure that the power keys will always be available when you begin painting by checking the Power Keys box on the User Preferences card in the Home stack. See Appendix B for a list of all the power keys.

Line Size, Brush Shape, and Polygon Sides

These call up the dialog boxes shown earlier in this chapter.

Edit Pattern

This summons the dialog box in Figure 6-18. (You can also call up this dialog box by double-clicking on any pattern in the Patterns palette.)

Figure 6-18. Edit Pattern Dialog Box

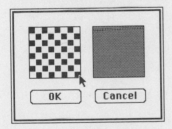

Use Edit Pattern to create custom patterns. The left-hand box is a FatBits representation of the selected pattern. You'll notice that it is eight pixels on a side; all the patterns in the Patterns palette are based on the same 64-square matrix. On the right is how the pattern looks in normal scale. Click on any black pixel in the FatBits section to turn it white and on any white pixel to turn it black. To save your new pattern, click on OK. Try examining some of the more intricate patterns in the Patterns palette with Edit pattern; you'll see that all of them are really quite simple. You can change any of them to suit your needs.

An alternative way to create a new pattern is to base one on a drawing you've already made. Call up the Edit Pattern box and then click on any area in your drawing with the pointer. *HyperCard* will read an 8 × 8 pixel area around the point you clicked on and make it a pattern. Try this for yourself.

Draw Filled

Draw Filled does the same thing as double-clicking on the rectangle, rounded rectangle, oval, or irregular polygon—it makes the shape tools draw filled with the current pattern.

Draw Centered (power key C) and Draw Multiple (power key M)

Use Draw Centered to draw a shape with a shape tool so that it is centered over a chosen point. With Draw Centered on, for example, rectangles will expand from the center rather than from one corner as you create them.

Draw Multiple leaves traces as you create a shape—as you can see in Figure 6-19. It is most useful used in combination with Draw Centered; with both options on at once you can effortlessly draw concentric circles, squares, and other shapes.

To draw concentric circles, squares, and other shapes:
1. Select the Hexagon polygon tool.
2. Choose Draw Centered and Draw Multiple
3. Drag back and forth and turn the hexagon around on its center.

Draw Centered and Draw Multiple have no effect on the Pencil, Brush, Spray, Curve, Bucket, or Freeform Polygon tools.

Figure 6-19. Draw Centered and Draw Multiple

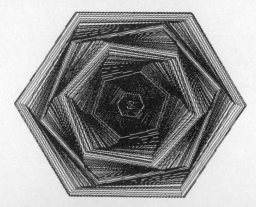

Double-Clicking the Tools

You've already seen that double-clicking on most of the painting tool icons changes the state of the tool or calls up a dialog box. Table 6-1 summarizes the effects of double-clicking.

Table 6-1. Double-Clicking the Paint Tools

Tool	Effect of Double-Clicking
Brush	Displays Brush Shapes box.
Bucket	Turns Pattern palette on-off.
Curve	Turns Draw Filled on-off.
Eraser	Clears picture.
Lasso	Lassos all.
Line	Displays Line Size box.
Oval	Turns Draw Filled on-off.
Graphic Text	Displays Text Style box.
Pattern	Displays Pattern Edit box.
Pencil	Turns FatBits on-off.
Polygon	Turns Draw Filled on-off.
Regular Polygon	Displays Polygon Sides box.
Rectangle	Turns Draw Filled on-off.
Round Rectangle	Turns Draw Filled on-off.
Selection	Selects all.

More on Graphics Keys

The Command, Option, and Shift keys can be used to modify the action of the painting tools. Table 6-2 summarizes the action of each key.

Table 6-2. Using Command, Option, and Shift

Tool	Drag w/ Command key	Drag w/ Option key	Drag w/ Shift key
Brush	Erases		Paints horizontally or vertically only
Curve		Draws w/ patterned border	
Eraser	Erases white		Erases horizontally or vertically only
Lasso	Lassos all	Copies selection	Moves selection horizontally or vertically only
Line		Draws w/pattern	Draws 15-degree angles
Oval		Draws w/ patterned border	Draws circle
Pencil	Toggles FatBits on-off		Draws horizontally or vertically only
Polygon		Draws w/pattern	Draws 15-degree angles
Rectangle		Draws w/ patterned border	Draws square
Regular Polygon		Draws w/ patterned border	Rotates by 15 degrees
Rounded Rectangle		Draws w/ patterned border	Draws rounded square
Selection	Selects close to shape	Copies selection	Moves selection horizontally or vertically only
Spray	Paints w/ erasing spray		Sprays horizontally or vertically only

Tools, menu options, keypresses, and dragging can be combined to create special graphics effects. Try painting with various tools and features active at the same time. For example, see what happens if you work with Draw Multiple and the Grid from the Options menu while using the Oval tool and pressing the Shift key. Experiment for yourself to see what other unusual and useful effects you can achieve.

Card Layouts

The last section in this chapter is purely visual—it shows you a number of ideas for using graphics to lay out your cards and enhance their appearance.

Figure 6-20. Sample Graphics

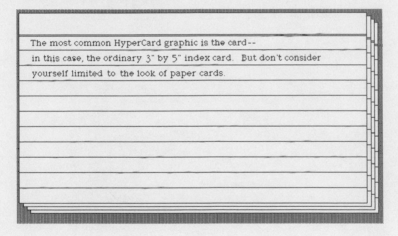

The most common HyperCard graphic is the card--
in this case, the ordinary 3" by 5" index card. But don't consider
yourself limited to the look of paper cards.

Figure 6-21. Sample Graphics 2

Figure 6-22. Sample Graphics 3

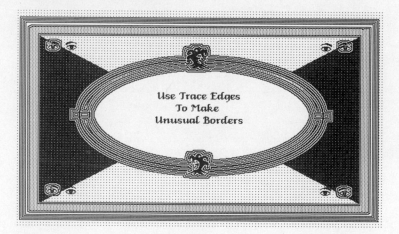

Figure 6-23. Sample Graphics 4

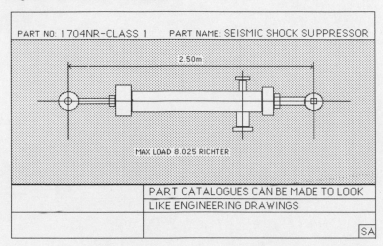

Figure 6-24. Sample Graphics 5

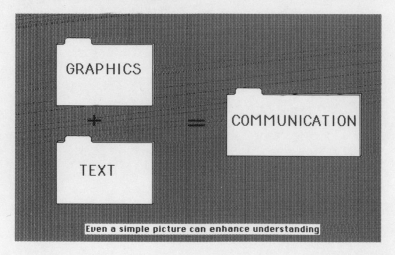

Chapter 7
Designing Your Own Stacks

Chapter 7
Designing Your Own Stacks

This chapter is a step-by-step tutorial designed to help you create your own stack for keeping family records. You'll be using the authoring skills you learned in the last two chapters—making and manipulating backgrounds, cards, fields, and buttons, creating links, and using the painting tools. In addition, you'll try your hand at creating some simple button scripts.

The Ideas Stacks

The Ideas disk supplied in the *HyperCard* package is a gold mine of readymade parts, pictures, and templates that you can use freely in your own creations. If you haven't looked through these stacks before, take a moment to browse through them now—your imagination is bound to be stimulated.

Art Ideas contains nearly 1000 pictures and symbols that you can cut out and paste onto other cards (see Figure 7-1 for an example). You'll find nearly every symbol and image you could need for most *HyperCard* design work. It's also possible to import art in the MacPaint file format from other programs and clip art collections (see Appendix A for more on importing and exporting graphics).

Figure 7-1. Art Ideas Sample

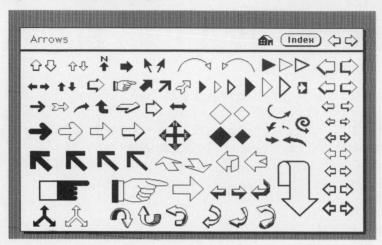

Button Ideas (Figure 7-2) stores a wide variety of buttons, complete with functions attached. Go to the stack now and try some of the unfamiliar buttons—don't miss "Bill Sez."

Figure 7-2. Button Ideas

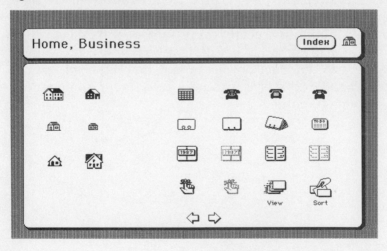

Card Ideas has eyecatching sample cards. You'll find the maps and ruler cards particularly useful (see Figure 7-3).

Figure 7-3. Card Ideas

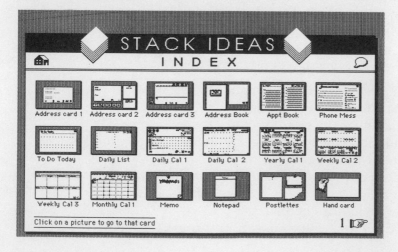

Stack Ideas contains 72 backgrounds to use as the basis for new stacks. All of them can be readily modified to suit your needs. Figure 7-4 shows a page of the Stack Ideas index.

Figure 7-4. Stack Ideas

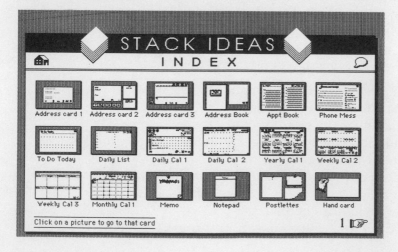

In this tutorial we'll be using material from the Stack Ideas, Card Ideas, and Art Ideas stacks.

Planning the Stack

Designing your own stack takes the same kind of planning and preparation that you might invest in designing and building a piece of furniture or any other construction project.

Set Your Goal. First, be sure you have a clear idea of the task you want your stack to perform. Analyze your goal and ask these questions:

• What job do you need the stack to do?
• What general features should the stack have?
• Can it do the job better than the method you are using now?
• Who will be using the stack?
• Should the stack be protected or restricted to the browsing level?
• What kind of look or style should the stack display?

The stack you'll be creating, Family Records, stores information on four typical areas that families keep records: automobile repair, monthly budget, household possessions, and emergency phone numbers. Each area will have a separate background, but all four areas will be linked together. This stack offers the usual advantages of *HyperCard* information management, plus a few special features.

Make a Stack Blueprint. Any complex project is made easier if you have a blueprint or diagram to follow. Among the questions drawing a blueprint will answer:

• Exactly how should information be arranged in the stack?
• What information is needed on each card?
• Will one background do, or are several required?
• Should individual buttons and fields be placed on backgrounds or on cards?
• What graphics are needed, and how will they help the design?
• Where will links be placed?
• Which objects will need scripts written for them?

Take a piece of paper and sketch it all out, or use *HyperCard*'s graphics tools to create a more polished blueprint. You'll find a sketch of immense help later, especially if the stack is complex. Figure 7-5 is a diagram of the Family Records stack.

Figure 7-5. Family Records Blueprint

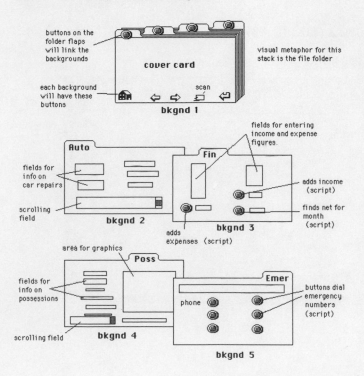

Gather Your Materials

Chances are you'll want to base your stack on readymade designs in the Ideas stacks or on other stacks you've collected. This can save you valuable time. In particular, you'll be returning again and again to Art Ideas and Stack Ideas for material. In this stack, you'll be using the following readymade parts:

• Lateral Files 2 (card ID 53760) from Stack Ideas (Figure 7-6).

Figure 7-6. Lateral Files 2

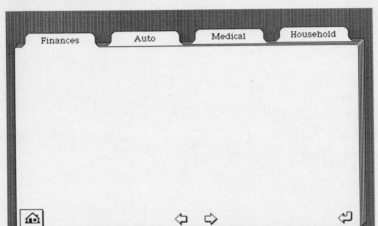

- The large house on card ID 10471 in Art Ideas (Figure 7-7).

Figure 7-7. House from Art Ideas

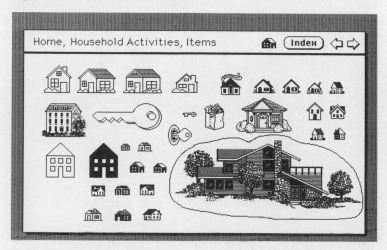

- The top of the Emergency card (card ID 23959) from Card Ideas (Figure 7-8).

Figure 7-8. Emergency Card

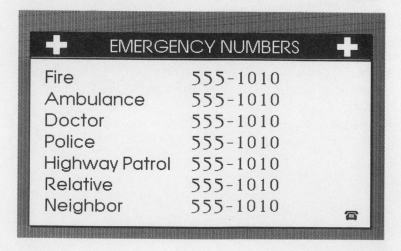

Although you won't need to do it for this stack, it's a good idea to copy small objects you plan to use in your stack as you come across them. Paste them onto a blank card in the stack you create so you'll have easy access to them as you're building the stack.

Creating the Stack

As you begin to actually make the stack, you should work from the most general elements—establishing the stack and backgrounds—to the most particular—buttons and links.

Step 1. Establish the Stack

Before you begin, make sure you are working with copies of the Ideas stacks. You'll also find it saves time if you tear off the Tools palette and position it in a convenient place on the screen, where you can get quick access to any tool.

To make copies of stacks:
1. Go to the Lateral Files 2 card (ID 53760) in Stack Ideas. This card will provide part of the background design for your new stack.
2. Click on the field tool. Delete the fields you see on the folder tabs along the top.
3. Click on the button tool. Delete the button you see along the top of the folder tabs. (You'll be adding buttons of your own later.)
4. Go to the Collection Catalog card (ID 69889) in Stack Ideas. Copy the Scan button. Return to the Lateral Files 2 card, and paste the button at the bottom right.
5. Copy this card. Figure 7-9 shows how it looks now.

Figure 7-9. Modified Lateral Files 2

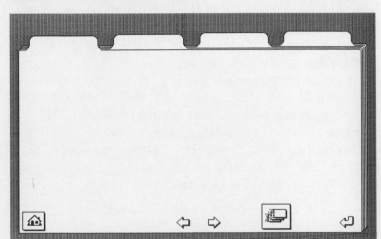

6. Choose New Stack from the File menu.
7. Name the new stack *Family Records.* Copy the current background.
8. Save the new stack to the current folder and disk or to a data disk. Used regularly, this stack will grow in size, so you may want to give it its own disk.

Step 2. Set Up the Basic Backgrounds
This stack is a heterogeneous stack, with five backgrounds. All the backgrounds are based on the Lateral Files 2 background.

To set up the backgrounds:
1. You should be in your new stack. Call up the Background Info dialog box and name this background *Cover.* Note the background ID number.
2. Here's a trick. Enter background mode (Command-B) and click on the Pencil tool. Make a small dot on the background, somewhere inconspicuous—a single pixel is all that's required.

3. Paste the Lateral Files 2 card again into this stack (it should still be on the Clipboard). Now check Background Info for this new card. Name it *Automobile.* It has a new background ID number, different from the Cover background ID. If you hadn't made the small mark on the Cover background, the Automobile background would have had been pasted in with the same ID—meaning you would not have been able to modify one of the backgrounds without automatically modifying the other.
4. Repeat this process three more times. Name the new backgrounds *Financial, Possessions,* and *Emergency.* Don't forget to make a mark on each background you create.

You now have a stack with five nearly identical backgrounds.

Step 3. Make a Cover for the Stack
The first card in this stack will be a cover card.

To make a cover card:
1. Call up the Card Info dialog box. Name this card *Family Records Cover 1.*
2. Go to card ID 10471 in Art Ideas. Use the Lasso to select the big house picture, and copy it to the Clipboard.
3. Return to the Cover card.
4. Reenter background mode.
5. Paste the house onto the Cover card as shown in Figure 7-10.
6. Use the Line tool to draw a line under the leftmost folder tab, as shown in the figure. This indicates that the folders are still closed.
7. Use the Graphic Text tool to add the title Family Records. The font used was Geneva, 18-point, bold, with an extra space between each letter. After you've typed out the text, use the Select tool to move it to the exact location. See Figure 7-10.

Figure 7-10. Family Records Cover 1

Step 4. Make the Automobile Background
Next, work on the Automobile part of the stack. This card helps you keep track of your car repair outlays.

To make an Automobile background:
1. Go to the second card in the stack. Name it *Auto Card 1*.
2. Enter background mode. You'll be laying out the background fields first.
3. Choose New Field in the Objects menu. Select the field that appears and give it the following properties: transparent, show lines, Geneva 12 font, 16 line spacing, align left.
4. Use this first field to make all the fields shown in Figure 7-11. Clone the field by pressing the Option key as you drag. Press the Shift key at the same time to constrain the movement of the cloned field, so that you can align it easily with the other fields. First do the fields on the left.
5. Now make a scrolling field. It should have all the other properties of the first new field. Position it at the bottom left.
6. Add the fields on the right.

7. Check the field layer order by choosing the browse tool and tabbing from field to field. The tab should progress from upper left to lower right. Use Bring Closer and Send Farther to adjust the order of any field that may be out of place.
8. Now add graphic text as in Figure 7-11. Use Geneva 12, bold, 16 line spacing, and align left. After you've typed the labels, use the Selection tool with the constraining Shift key to position them precisely. Also, add the folder tab label at upper left. It's in Chicago 12-point.

The Automobile background at this stage is shown in Figure 7-11.

Figure 7-11. Auto Background 1

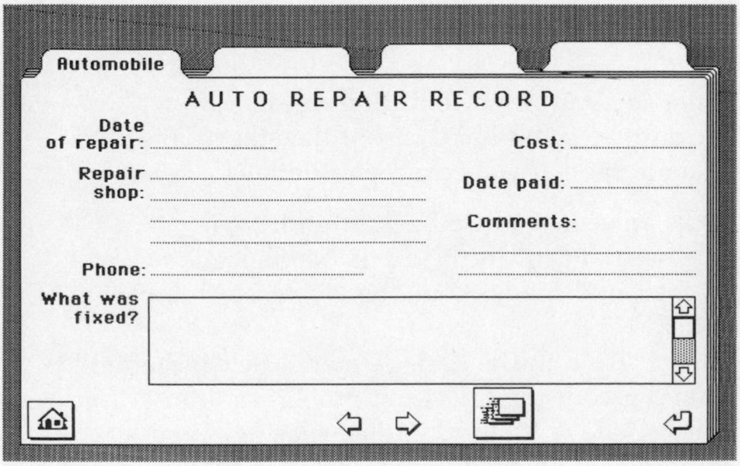

Step 5. Make the Financial Background

This is a monthly budget card that tallies your income and expenses.

To make the Financial background:

1. Go to the third card in the stack. Name it *Financial Card 1*.
2. Enter background mode. You'll be laying out the background fields first.
3. Choose the field tool and New Field. When a field appears, give it these properties: transparent, show lines, Geneva 14 font, bold, align left.
4. Resize the field down to one line height and clone it. Move

both fields to the upper right. You'll be adjusting their size again later.

5. Create another new field. Give it these properties: shadow, no lines shown, Chicago 12 font (these fields will be holding dollar amounts, and Chicago has particularly readable numerals), align right.

6. Shrink the field to the size shown and position it at the top of the left-hand column. Use the Option-Shift-drag combination to clone and align ten fields on the left and six fields on the right, spaced as shown in Figure 7-12. Again, work from top left to bottom right, then check field order by tabbing through them as you did with the Automobile background.

7. Now add the background text. The title text at top is in Geneva 14 bold; the rest is in Geneva 12 plain. Use Select to move the text into position. Adjust the spacing and size of the fields as necessary. Add Financial to the leftmost folder tab in the Chicago 12 font.

The Financial background at this stage is shown in Figure 7-12. As you can see, there are some unlabeled fields. These will have buttons that you'll add later.

Figure 7-12. Financial Background 1

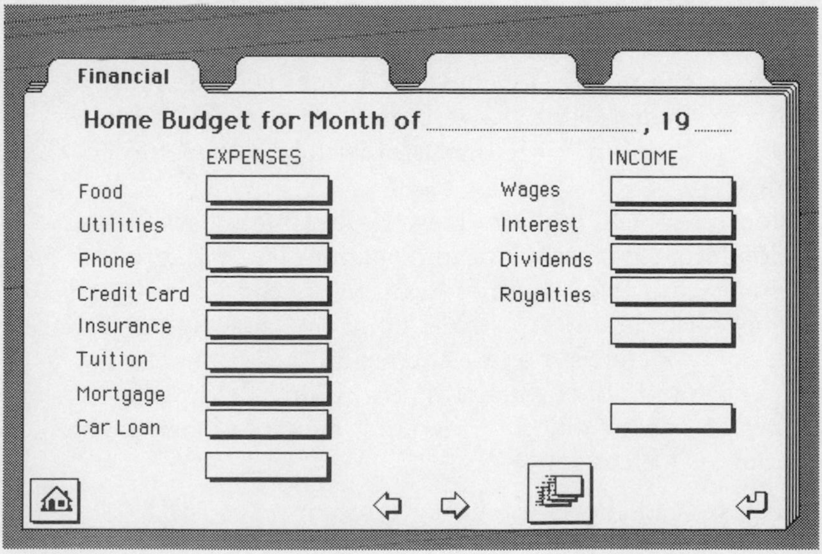

Step 6. Make the Possessions Background
This part of the stack is for keeping records on your household possessions for insurance or tax purposes. It includes an area for you to draw a picture of the item.

To make the Possessions background:
1. Go to the fourth card in the stack. Name it *Possessions Card 1*.
2. Enter background mode. You'll be laying out the background graphics first this time.
3. Choose the rectangle tool and a checkerboard pattern from the Patterns menu. Press 6 to set a wide line size. Draw a patterned rectangle on the right side of the background by pressing the Option key as you drag. Right inside the patterned rectangle, draw another in thin black (see Figure 7-13). Or create any other decorative border you like.
4. Make more room on the background by changing the button icons to smaller versions. Turn on the button tool and double-click on each button in turn. Click on Icon to get to the icon resource window, select the smallest available icon for that button, and click on OK. Note also that the Home and scan buttons have been changed from shadowed style to transparent to save screen clutter. As you add graphics and fields, move these buttons around to fit the developing design.
5. Now add the graphic text. The title of the card is in Geneva 14 bold; the rest is in Geneva 12 bold with 20-point line spacing. Remember to leave plenty of room for the fields. Add the label on the leftmost folder tab in the Chicago 12 font.
6. Choose the field tool and New Field. Create background fields for each category of information. Use background fields with these properties: transparent, no lines shown, Geneva 12 plain font with 16-point line spacing, align left. Figure 7-13 shows the text and field arrangement.
7. The bottom field on the left is a scrolling field for keeping notes on the condition of the equipment, or for other important information.

Figure 7.13 shows the background at this stage.

Figure 7-13. Possessions Background 1

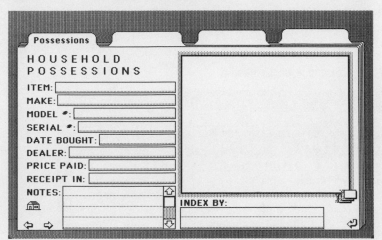

Step 7. Make the Emergency Background

With this card, you can automatically dial emergency numbers with a single mouse click (if your Mac is hooked up to a modem or an acoustic coupler).

To make the Emergency background:

1. Go to the fifth and last card in the stack. Name it *Emergency Card 1.*
2. Go to the Emergency card (ID 23959) in Card Ideas. Emergency Card 1 in Family Records is based on this card.
3. Enter background mode. Click on the Selection tool. Carefully select the top of this card, the part that says *Emergency.* Copy the selection to the Clipboard.
4. Return to Emergency Card 1 in Family Records. Enter background mode. Carefully paste the picture in at top, as shown in Figure 7-14. Clean up the edges in FatBits with the Eraser, if necessary.
5. Using graphic text, add the names of emergency numbers (substitute your own for the ones in the figure). Arrange

them in descending order of importance. The text in Figure
7-14 is in Geneva 14 bold with 20-point spacing. Don't forget to add the word *Emergency* in Chicago 12 on the leftmost folder tab.

Figure 7-14. Emergency Background 1

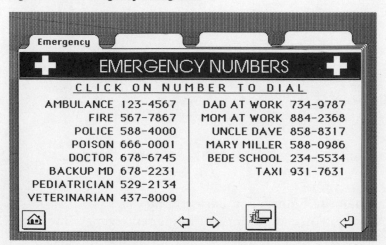

Step 8. Add Buttons with Links.

Now that the field and graphic layout of the backgrounds is
complete, it's time to add the custom buttons and links. You
need buttons on the folder tabs to get you from one part of
the stack to another, and you need a couple specialized buttons that will introduce you to HyperTalk script writing.

To add custom buttons and links:

1. Go to the Cover card. Enter background mode.
2. Click on the button tool and choose New Button from the
   Objects menu.
3. Double-click on the button that appears to call up the Button Info dialog box. Name the button *Automobile* and give it
   the following properties: transparent, show name, auto-
   hilite on, no icon.
4. Link this button to Auto Card 1 using the Link To feature.
   Click on Link To; go to Auto Card 1; click on This Card.

5. Repeat this process with three more background buttons, all cloned from the Automobile button. As with fields, clone the buttons by dragging them while pressing the Option key. Name these buttons *Financial, Possessions,* and *Emergency,* and then link them to their respective cards.

6. Position the buttons on the Cover card folder tabs as in Figure 7-15. Copy the buttons in turn and paste them on the tabs of the other backgrounds. The figure shows how they should be arranged. Note that you only need three tab buttons for the backgrounds (except on the Cover) because the tab for the current background is already labeled with graphic text.

7. Activate the browse tool and test the buttons to make sure you've got the links right.

Figure 7-15. Folder Tab Buttons

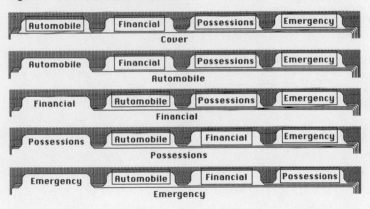

Step 9. Create Scripted Buttons for the Financial Background

Now you need to make three buttons on the Financial background. These buttons will add your monthly expenses and income with just two clicks, and then they will calculate your net income for the month with a third. The catch is you have to type in HyperTalk scripts for each button. (If you like, you can skip ahead to the next two chapters, which discuss HyperTalk scripting in detail, and then come back to this chapter.)

To make buttons on the Financial background:
1. Go to the Financial card. Enter background mode.
2. Create a background button. Name it *Total 1*, and give it these properties: round rectangle, name visible, auto-hilite, no icon.
3. The purpose of this button is to add your expenses. Another way of thinking of it is that the button is going to add the values you enter into the expenses fields and put the total into the field at bottom left. That's almost exactly what the script is going to say.
4. Click on Script in the Button Info dialog box to get to the script editing window. Already entered are the terms *on mouseUp* and *end mouseUp*. These just tell the button to act on the script when you click on the button's active area.
5. Type in the script exactly as shown in Figure 7-16. (All the Mac's standard text-editing features work in the script window, except the menus aren't active; use keyboard commands instead.) You should have no difficulty understanding what the script is telling the button to do. There are two things you should note. The character at the end of the second line of the script is a *soft return*, which you make by typing Option-Return. Use this when a script line is getting too long for the script window but you don't want to hit the Return key alone, which ends the script line and sets up for a new command. The other thing to note is that, although this script refers to the fields by their field numbers, you can just as easily (and perhaps more safely) refer to fields by their names or ID numbers.
6. When you are finished typing, click OK.
7. Move this button next to the bottom left field and test it out by entering some figures into the expenses fields and clicking on the button. Don't type in numbers with commas separating the thousands (as in $14,000); *HyperCard* won't know how to interpret those. If you get an error message or the button doesn't work right, go back to the script and check that it's typed in correctly.

    You also need a background button for the Income side of the background. You can use a clone of the Total button. Call this new button *Total 2*.

Figure 7-16. Total 1 Button Script

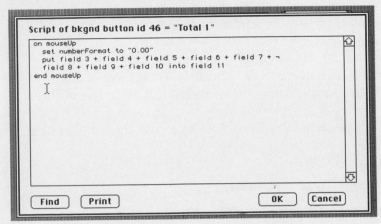

```
Script of bkgnd button id 46 = "Total 1"

on mouseUp
  set numberFormat to "0.00"
  put field 3 + field 4 + field 5 + field 6 + field 7 + ¬
  field 8 + field 9 + field 10 into field 11
end mouseUp
  I
```

Find   Print   OK   Cancel

8. Click on Script to go to the script window for this button. Enter the script in Figure 7-17.
9. Position the button next to the field second from the bottom on the right.
10. Test the button.

Figure 7-17. Total 2 Script Window.

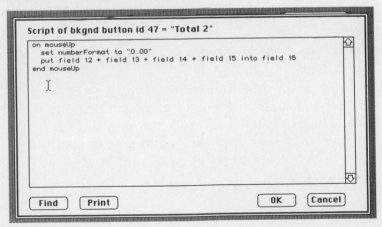

```
Script of bkgnd button id 47 = "Total 2"

on mouseUp
  set numberFormat to "0.00"
  put field 12 + field 13 + field 14 + field 15 into field 16
end mouseUp
  I
```

Find   Print   OK   Cancel

137

The last button will tell you what's left over (if anything) after the month's outlays. In other words, it will subtract total expenses from total income, and then will display the result.

11. Again, you can use a clone of the Total button. However, you should name this new button *Net Income or Loss*.

12. Enter the script window for this button and type in the script shown in Figure 7-18.

13. Resize the button and position it next to the bottom right field.

14. Test the button.

Figure 7-18. Net Income or Loss Script

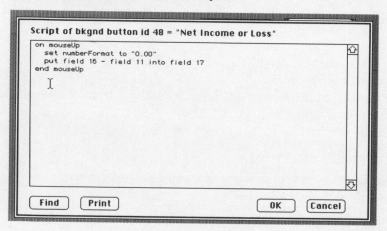

```
Script of bkgnd button id 48 = "Net Income or Loss"

on mouseUp
  set numberFormat to "0.00"
  put field 16 - field 11 into field 17
end mouseUp
```

Find   Print   OK   Cancel

Now that you've made three buttons, you may be wondering whether you could make one button that does the work of all of them. In fact, you can. Simply combine all three scripts into one, and assign it to the Net Income or Loss button. Try this as an exercise in script writing on your own.

Step 10. Create Dialing Buttons for the Emergency Background

It's time to add instant dialing buttons to the Emergency card. These will enable you or anyone in your family to dial a number on the card without having to type it into the message box or even select it (that is, if your Mac is hooked up to a modem or an acoustic coupler).

To add instant dialing buttons:

1. Go to Emergency Card 1 and enter background mode.
2. Choose the button tool and create a new button with these properties: transparent, no name shown, no icon, auto hilite.
3. Go to the script window and type in one of the following scripts between on mouseUp and end mouseUp:

dial " "   **--if you have an acoustic coupler**
dial " " with modem   **--if you have a modem**

     Add modem dialing codes as appropriate in quotation marks at the end of the line. For example, if you have a Hayes-compatible modem, you would type:

dial " " with modem "ATDT"

4. Move and size the button so that it encloses the first name and number (in this case, *Ambulance*).
5. Clone this button (with Option-Shift-drag) and put one over every name and number, as in Figure 7-19.
6. For each button, enter the script window and type in the number the button is for between the quotation marks. For example, the complete script for the Ambulance button reads

on mouseUp
    dial "1234567"
end mouseUp

7. Test each button, listening for dial tones.

Figure 7-19. Emergency Dialing Buttons

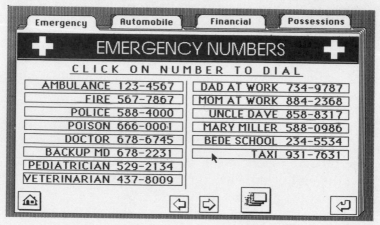

Step 11. Make a Button for the Home Card
The final touch for any important new stack is to include a button for the stack on the Home card.

To create a button for the Home Card:
1. Go to the Cover card.
2. Copy it to the Clipboard.
3. Go to the Home card.
4. Press Command-Shift-V. This pastes a miniature picture of the card on the Clipboard onto the Home card. Move the miniature picture into a clear spot. Use graphic text to label it *Family Records* using Geneva 9-point type.
5. Create a card button named *Family Records*. It should have these characteristics: transparent, no name shown, no auto-hilite, no icon. Link this button to the Cover card.
6. Move and size this button so that it fits over the miniature picture of the Cover card on the Home card, as in Figure 7-20.
7. Test the link.

Figure 7-20. Family Records Button

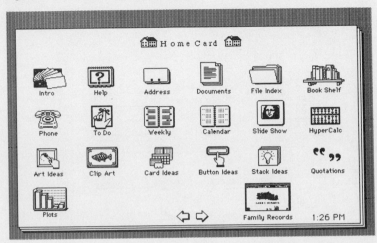

Figures 7-21, 7-22, and 7-23 show how the Automobile, Financial, and Possessions cards look with information entered.

Figure 7-21. Automobile Card

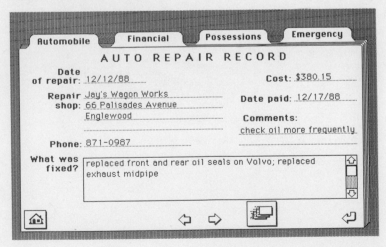

Figure 7-22. Financial Card

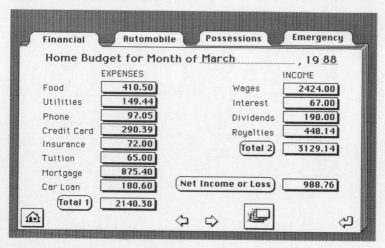

Figure 7-23. Possessions Card

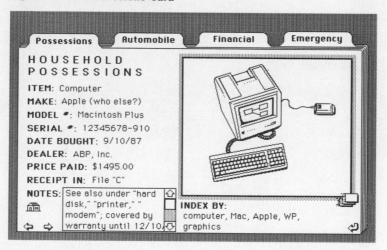

Using the Stack

Create blank versions of the Auto Repair, Financial, and Possessions cards by using the New Card command in the Edit menu. You'll want to do this each month for the Financial cards, for example.

On the Financial cards, you may want to add additional categories of income or expenses, such as a bonus or estimated taxes payments, from time to time. These can be added as card fields. Be sure to revise the button scripts if you do. As an alternative, you might want to add a few blank fields to the background; then use them as necessary. Again, you'll need to revise the script to look for any contents of these additional fields.

One way to use the Possessions cards is to fill in the text information on an object you own, then print the card and attach a photograph of the object. This saves the time and effort of drawing the object, and it's more acceptable as proof of ownership to your insurance company or the IRS.

If you use New Card to copy the Emergency card, you'll get an exact duplicate of the original, because everything, including the text, is on the background. Instead, use the make-a-mark technique described in Step 2 above to copy the Emergency card background. Then you can change the new background without affecting the original. You can simply erase all the names and numbers on the graphics layer, add new ones in the same places, and then change the numbers in the button scripts.

Family Records is not by any means a very sophisticated stack. It was designed primarily to give you practice in applying basic authoring concepts. There are probably a thousand ways the stack could be made more functional, or even completely redesigned. For example, make it four linked stacks instead of one stack with five backgrounds. If variations occur to you, by all means try them. At the very least, you should tailor the numbers and titles of fields to suit your own information needs.

Some Suggested Applications for *HyperCard*

The number of possible applications for *HyperCard* is enormous. The stacks supplied with *HyperCard* should give you some ideas of your own. Other uses for the program were suggested in the first chapter of this book. Following is a list of more possible applications for education, business, and creative use.

Business

Animatics (animated storyboards for advertising)
Business library catalogs
Custom databases
Custom forms of all kinds
Custom labels
Custom spreadsheets
Design of all kinds
Desktop presentations
Directories
Employee forms and records
Hypermedia newsletters and corporate publications
Hypermedia reports
Individual expense forms and records
Insurance forms and records
Interactive training
Inventory forms and records
Macintosh training
Macintosh utilities
Mailing lists
Note taking and note organization
Online help systems
Order froms and records
Outlining and planning
Point-of-sale demonstrations
Product catalogs
Purchasing forms and records
Sales forms and records
Software development
Timesheets
Video promotions

Education
> Art and music instruction
> Educational records
> Flash cards
> Hypermedia tests and term papers
> Interactive training of all kinds
> Macintosh training
> Preschool education
> Programming instruction
> Remedial reading and writing
> Research database access (videodisk, mainframe)
> Research organization
> School library cataloging
> Science and math instruction
> Special education
> Student publications and stackware
> Term paper outlining
> Vocational training

Creative
> Alternate Mac interfaces
> Amateur programming of all kinds
> Animated cartoons
> Collection catalogs
> Film scoring
> Film storyboards
> Games and adventures
> Graphics utilities
> Hypermedia art
> Hypermedia comic strips
> Hypermedia stories, poetry, novels, and drama
> Music editing
> Music videos

Chapter 8
Overview of HyperTalk

Chapter 8
Overview of HyperTalk

If you've worked through the book this far, you've already used HyperTalk, *HyperCard*'s programming language. You've entered HyperTalk instructions into the message box and have typed in HyperTalk scripts for buttons. In this chapter, you'll take a more systematic look at the concepts behind HyperTalk.

What Is a Programming Language?

Most *HyperCard* users have never used a programming language nor written a computer program. You may be wondering what a programming language is, and how to use one.

A programming language is primarily a way to communicate with your computer. Just as you use English to talk to another person, you use a programming language to "talk" to the computer and give it instructions.

Imagine that the only way you can communicate with a friend is by reading him or her words out of a book. You can't speak your own words, only those in the book, and only in the order the author has written them. Even if it's a great book, you won't be able to find many things you want to say.

If you don't know a programming language, you're in an analogous situation with respect to your computer. The only way you can communicate with your Macintosh is through an application program written by someone else. While the application may be very useful, it's not likely to meet your needs exactly. There will be many things you'd like the program to do that it can't. But, since you have no independent way to communicate with and command your computer, you're restricted to using only the tools the application provides.

Knowing a programming language gives you the power to make your computer do just the things you want it to do. The problem has been, however, that programming languages, even relatively simple ones like BASIC or Logo, are difficult to learn, and even more awkward to write. And the Macintosh, with its complex operating system, is notoriously difficult to program. So the majority of Macintosh users have been content to use the applications that are available, leaving the programming to professionals.

HyperTalk should do much to change that situation. As programming languages go, it is easy to learn. Writing a HyperTalk script is as close to writing standard English as programming gets. And, HyperTalk protects you from the nitpicking complexities of commanding the Macintosh. It takes care of all the details, leaving you only the task (perhaps it will become a pleasure) of crafting a well-made script.

One thing to note is that HyperTalk is not a universal programming language, like BASIC or Pascal. In its present form, it can only be used within *HyperCard*, and only on the Macintosh. It is possible to create links between HyperTalk and any other language that runs on the Macintosh, but that's for advanced programmers and is beyond the scope of this book.

What Scripting Can Do

You know that a lot of useful *HyperCard* work can be done without any knowledge of HyperTalk, but you've also seen some of the power that HyperTalk *scripts*—the series of instructions that define the characteristics, purpose, and action of a *HyperCard* object—can give your stacks. Without basic script-writing skills, you'll be limited to what the authoring tools can accomplish for you, or to scripts that have been written by others. But what exactly can you do with scripts?

Scripts can link objects one to another. For example, instead of using the Link To feature in the Button Info box to link a button to a distant card, you can write a script for the button that says "go to card 1."

Scripts can perform any menu action, keyboard command, or mouse action. You can easily write a button script that copies the current card to another location, that prints out the contents of a particular field, that draws a straight line across the screen, or that does any other action you would normally initiate from menu, keyboard, or mouse. Scripts can also be used to call up custom dialog boxes.

Scripts can get text information from anywhere in the stack and display it in a field. You can program a card to find the contents of a field elsewhere in the stack and put it into a field on the current card.

Scripts can supply information about the condition of the Macintosh system. For example, a card script can put the current time or date (derived from the Mac's internal clock and calendar) into a field on a card whenever you open the card.

Scripts can perform mathematical or other operations on field information. You did just that with the Financial button scripts in the last chapter. These operations can be quite complex, chaining many calculations to get a result that would take a lot of work to arrive at by hand.

Scripts can wait for you to enter a particular piece of information, and then take one of a number of actions based on what you've entered. This has many implications for educational programming. For example, in an educational stack, you can script a field to look for a particular answer from a student. If the student types in the wrong answer, the stack can "branch" to a different version of the lesson that helps the student understand his or her mistake.

To get an even better idea of what scripts can do, a good place to begin is *HyperCard*'s Help stacks. As you roam through Help, try out fields and buttons, and then check the object's script to get a sense of how each effect was accomplished.

How Scripts Work

In HyperTalk, you write scripts for objects—in programmer's lingo, HyperTalk is an *object-oriented programming language*. (As you'll recall, *HyperCard* has five classes of objects: buttons, fields, backgrounds, cards, and stacks.) If you imagine each *HyperCard* object to be an actor in the program, the object's script is what tells it when to come onstage, how to move, what lines to speak, and when to exit.

Any object can have its own script, but many objects, you'll discover, have no scripts—and don't need them. Scripts can't exist independently of objects. When you copy an object that has a script, the script is copied, too. In that sense, a script is another property of the object, like the text style of a field.

Scripts are not interdependent (unless you write them to be). The action of one script does not depend on the action of another, just as you can have fields and buttons that are completely independent of each other. That means that if there is an error in the script of one object, that error won't necessarily have an impact on the script of any other object. Likewise, a change that you make in one script generally won't affect other scripts. This modularity makes it easy to test, modify, and debug (that is, find and fix the mistakes in) scripts. And, you can add a new scripted object to a stack or delete one that already exists at any time. This is different from the situation in BASIC and most programming languages, which require that you write a program that runs straight through from beginning to end. Programs in these languages are difficult to modify and debug, because a change in any line of the program may affect other lines in unpredictable ways.

Scripts and Messages

A message is any kind of internal *HyperCard* communication. You've used the message box to send HyperTalk messages to *HyperCard*, such as "go last." In fact, the main activity of *HyperCard* is sending messages to objects, which it does constantly (most of these are idle messages about the current condition of the Mac and *HyperCard*). *HyperCard* is like a complex communications network, with messages passing back and forth among all the objects in the program, and to and from *HyperCard* itself.

Unlike messages in the message box, which execute as soon as you end the message by hitting the Return or the Enter key, scripts are passive until some message triggers them. In the case of a button, for example, the event that usually triggers the script is clicking on the button. What happens behind the scenes is that *HyperCard* detects the mouse click on the area of the button and sends a mouseUp system message (see below) to the button. This is intercepted by the button, and it initiates the action of the script. (The button knows to respond to a mouseUp message because its script is written to look for such a message—most button scripts begin on mouseUp.) Once the script is triggered, it takes the action described in the script—and this always involves sending another message, usually an instruction, either to another object or to *HyperCard* itself. The part of a script that looks for and acts on a message is called the *message handler*.

Messages and the Object Hierarchy

Messages are routed through *HyperCard* along a set *hierarchy*. This hierarchy is like a ladder of *HyperCard* objects. The hierarchy begins at the bottom rung with buttons and fields and progresses to the card, the background, the stack, the Home stack, and finally, at the top rung, to *HyperCard* itself. This arrangement of levels should already feel natural to you, since you went down the hierarchy as you were making the exercise stack in the last chapter.

The hierarchy works like this. When *HyperCard* first detects an event, such as a mouse click, it passes a mouseUp system message to the object under the browse tool. If that object, let's say it's a button, has the proper message handler (a script that begins *on mouseUp*), the message is received, and the script is triggered.

What happens if the button does not have the proper message handler? In that case, the button can't receive the message, and it is bounced back to *HyperCard. HyperCard* then tries to pass the message to the next rung up the ladder. If that object, a card, also doesn't have the proper message handler, then the message continues on up the hierarchy until it meets an object with the proper message handler. Eventually, the message may reach the top rung, *HyperCard* itself. If *HyperCard* doesn't know how to receive the message, then the message is declared null and void, and *HyperCard* begins waiting for the next event. Figure 8-1 diagrams the *HyperCard* hierarchy and how messages are passed up the ladder.

Figure 8-1. *HyperCard* Hierarchy

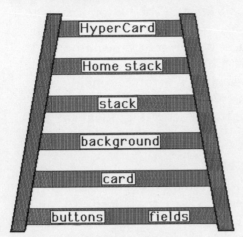

Not all messages start at the bottom rung. *HyperCard* knows to send certain messages immediately to the correct rung on the ladder. The instruction to create a new card, for example, is sent directly to the card rung.

The concept of hierarchy has a direct bearing on how you will write scripts and to which objects you'll assign them. It's especially important to assign a message handler to the proper rung in the hierarchy. This issue tends to arise when you are trying to decide whether to put a message handler in a script for a card, a background, a stack, or the Home stack. For example, you could assign all your message handlers to your Home stack. *HyperCard* will find them there, sooner or later, but it will slow down the program's operation considerably. It's much better HyperTalk programming practice to assign a message handler to the lowest rung where it will still operate successfully. Keep in mind the function of the script you are writing. Do you want it to affect every stack? Put it in the Home stack. Should it change every card in the current stack? Write the script for the background, if the stack has only one background, or for the stack, if there is more than one background.

HyperTalk Grammar and Vocabulary

One of the first things you notice about HyperTalk, as mentioned above, is that it is a lot like English. Every term in HyperTalk is an English word or is derived from English, like *mouseUp.* You can use English grammar to guide you in writing a HyperTalk sentence. For example, *Go to the last card of the "Home" stack* is a completely legitimate sentence in English and in HyperTalk, and it means the same thing in both languages. But HyperTalk is more forgiving grammatically than English. *Go card 5* is poor English, but good HyperTalk—in fact, it's better HyperTalk than the first example because it's more efficient to type.

HyperTalk is able to understand any number of ways to say the same thing, as long as the statement conforms to a few general syntactical and structural rules. HyperTalk is also unconcerned with things such as proper capitalization and the number of spaces between words. Even in a HyperTalk compound word like *mouseUp,* the capital *U* is only a convention. *Mouseup, mOuSeUp,* or *MOUSEuP* would work just as well. Many HyperTalk terms can be abbreviated; for example, you may use *loc* for *location, msg* for *message* or *message box,* and *rect* for *rectangle.*

You can use connecting words and prepositions just as in English. Words such as *to, before, into, after, of, by, this, contains,* and so on can be used in HyperTalk, making the writing of comprehensible scripts much easier.

Naming Objects

The names of objects function as the addresses in *HyperCard,* giving the program the information it needs to send script messages to the right place. Names can be written in a variety of ways. As noted in earlier chapters, you can specify an object in a script by its given name, object number, ID number, or, in the case of a card, position in the stack. For example, the names *TRex card, card 12, card id 12345,* or *next card* could all refer to the same card. But it's safest to refer to an object by its

ID number or given name because the object number or position of an object may change if you add or subtract another object from the stack, background, or card. One thing you should not do is start an object's given name with a number: 23skidoo.

If you need to use the name of an object that is not in the current stack, be sure to use the full pathname of the object—*card field 7 of card "TRex" of stack "Late Cretaceous."* (Always specify if you are referring to a card object in your script; otherwise *HyperCard* will look automatically for a background object.) The *of* tells *HyperCard* that there is more name to come.

Proper names, menu options (New Field), or text you want HyperTalk to treat just as text and not as a potential instruction, should be in quotation marks. As an example, you can type *Put "this is just text" into field 3* into your script, and the words *this is just text* will appear in the field. Typing *put this is just text into field 3* will just get you an error message. If you are specifying a menu option, make sure you type the entire name of the option, including an ellipsis if it has one—for example: doMenu "Card Info. . .".

Names can be even more specific than that when referring to the contents of fields. You can be as precise as you like—for example, *put character 1 of word 3 of line 1 of card field id 3456 of card "TRex" into bkgnd field "true or false."* This is very helpful when you are writing a script to alphabetize the contents of fields or when you want *HyperCard* to act on the entry of a particular letter or word into a field.

Statements

HyperTalk statements are always imperatives. The verb or action word (usually a command, see below) comes first, then the parameter, the name of what is to be acted on and any other conditions that are required. You can see this *command-parameter* construction in these typical HyperTalk statements:

Statement	Command	Parameter
go home	go	parameter
doMenu "New Field"	doMenu	"New Field" (the menu item that doMenu will activate)
set lockScreen to true	set	lockscreen to true
get the value of field 3	get	the value of field 3

A HyperTalk script is nothing more than a list of imperatives:

on mouseUp
   visual effect iris open
   go to next card of this background
   put the long date into field "Date"
   send mouseUp to button"Previous Total" **--that's like you**
                                                  --clicking on the
                                                  --the button--an
                                                  --example of a script
                                                  --sending a message
                                                  --to another object
end mouseUp

Commands

The HyperTalk vocabulary is divided into several classes of terms. The terms you'll be using most often are *commands*. A command is one of the instruction words such as go, find, put, sort, open, play, and so on. You are already quite familiar with many common commands. A good way to practice using new commands is with the message box. Try typing these into the message box, hitting Return or Enter at the end of each line to execute the command:

beep 10
print this card
play "boing"
doMenu "Open Stack ..."
ask "Do you want to go on?"

157

System Messages

Scripts are triggered by *system messages*, messages sent by *HyperCard* about the mouse, keyboard, and other actions within the program. A *trap* for a system message—on mouseUp, for example—opens every script. MouseUp, the message that the mouse button has been released, initiates the majority of button scripts and is probably the system message most familiar to you. There are, however, many others. For example, mouseEnter, mouseWithin, and mouseLeave detect the position of the pointer in relation to the boundaries of buttons and fields. Keystrokes are detected with system messages such as returnKey and arrowKey. And you can even detect events like the creation of new objects or the choice of a menu option, on newCard, for example.

Functions

A HyperTalk *function* is a term that asks for and retrieves the current state of a *HyperCard* or Macintosh activity. A function always returns a result in text or numbers, such as the current time and date or the number of characters in a text field. Try these functions in the message box:

the long date
the number of cards
the seconds
the ticks

Functions are often specified right after a command, for example

get the long date
put the seconds into field "Elapsed Time"

Function terms are usually preceded by the word *the*.

You can even define your own functions. All that's needed is for you to declare at the beginning of the message handler what the name of the new command or function is and what it means. See the next chapter for instructions on how to do this.

Operators

An operator is a mathematical function, such as $+$ (plus), $*$ (multiply), and $>$ (greater than). Like functions, operators return a value, such as a sum or the result of a comparison between two numbers. Try typing the following into the message box, hitting Return after each line:

put 3 into a
put 4 into b
put 5 into c

(*a*, *b*, and *c* are local variables, see below)

$a\hat{}2 + b\hat{}2 = c\hat{}2$

($\hat{}$ is the exponent symbol)

This should return the word *true*, meaning that a^2 (9) plus b^2 (16) does equal c^2 (25).

Control Structures

These are statements that make a decision or repeat an action with variations until a desired result is obtained. The most common control structures are **if ... then, else,** and **repeat.** (Variations on these are discussed in the next chapter.) Here is a script example of if . . . then:

```
on newCard
    get field 1
    if it is less than field 2 then
        add 2 to field 1
        subtract 2 from field 2
    end if
end newCard
```

The if . . . then part of the statement is testing whether a certain condition is true or false: in this case, whether the amount in field 1 is less than the amount in field 2. If the condition is true, if field 1 is less than field 2, the script then executes the next command lines, which add 2 to field 1 and subtract 2 from field 2. If the condition is false, field 1 is not less than field 2, the script skips to the next command on the same level as the if . . . then statement, ignoring the indented command. In essence, the script is making a decision to go one way or another based on information it gathers.

The command Add 2 to field 1 inside the if . . . then control structure would be indented automatically. This helps you read layers of control structures that are nested one within the next like matryushka dolls. Also note that the control structure has to be closed with "end if."

Note: Control structures cannot be tested in the message box.

Constants

A *constant* is a word that substitutes for a predefined value. HyperTalk constants can be used to enter values from the mouse and keyboard, such as up, down, quote, and return, or to test whether certain values are true or false. For example

if the shiftKey is down then go to next card
read from file "TRex" until return
if answer1 is false then go home

Answer1 is a variable (see below).

Usually you'll be using the true-false constants within if . . . then structures.

Properties

A property is any characteristic of a *HyperCard* object, such as its location. Properties can be *global* (that is, they can be shared by all objects in *HyperCard*), or very *narrow*, (for example, the name of a button). There is a HyperTalk term for every object property and for every painting property, for instance:

- set style of button "TRex" to transparent
- set textFont of field 1 to Chicago
- set the pattern to 22—patterns are numbered from top left

In most cases, you'll want to set or change the property of an object; the set command is the right command for this.

Variables and Containers

A *variable* is a temporary container for *HyperCard* information. Variables can be *local*, active only for the duration of the current message handler, or *global*, active until you specifically eliminate them.

Local variables can have any name you like. Here are two examples:

put field 1 into pastrami HyperCard will put the contents of field 1 into a local variable named *pastrami*.

put pastrami into field 2 The contents of local variable pastrami are put into field 2.

The pastrami variable exists only for the duration of the current handler; if you end the script and then try to access pastrami from another script, *HyperCard* won't remember what you are talking about.

It is used as the name for a local variable that is called for automatically by certain commands such as get, ask, and convert. For example, this command automatically puts the location of the button into the special local variable It:

get location of button id 234

You can then type

put it into field 3

to display the location coordinates in the field. Once you do that, It is emptied.

Global variables have a longer life. In fact, a global will last as long as you need it to, but you must specifically create it with the global command:

on mouseUp
    global janet   —creates global variable and names it janet
    put field 1 into Janet
    add field 2 to Janet
    subtract Janet from field 3
end mouseUp

The global variable Janet, which now consists of the sum of the contents of field 1 and field 2, is still available for use by any other message handler.

HyperCard information is often held in *containers*. A container holds information until it is asked for by a script. Examples of containers are fields with text in them; local and global variables; and the message box. All of these can hold information for use in a script. *HyperCard* treats the name of the variable as standing for the content of the variable (that's why you can type Add field 1 and field 2, and get the sum of the numbers in the fields—not two fields joined together into one).

Most containers are temporary holders. Local variables only hold information for the duration of the current message handler. Most other containers are emptied when you quit the program. Only the text in fields is saved to disk.

You can ask for information in a container by item—a piece of text set off by commas, such as part of an address—or by characters, words, and lines. For example, imagine a global variable that contains the text

Tyrannosaurus Rex, a theropod, weighed 8 tons

You can, for example, put *theropod* in the field with this command

put item 2 of global into field 1

If you write *put word 4 of global into field 1*, then the word *theropod* will appear in the field. If you want to retrieve more than one word from the container, use this formulation: Put word 5 to 7 of global into field 1; this would put *weighed 8 tons* into the field.

If you want to retrieve text from a container in a different order or arrangement, use the *concatenate* symbol, an ampersand (&). It works like this:

put char 1 of word 1 & word 2 of global into field 1

The above would put TRex into the field. You can concatenate as many items as you like; use a double ampersand— && —to put a space between the concatenated items.

See Chapter 9 for a dictionary of every HyperTalk term and its use.

Accessing and Editing HyperTalk Scripts

As you learned in the last chapter, you can edit the script of any object in the script editing window. This is accessible via a button in that object's Info dialog box. To bypass the Info dialog box and see the script of a button or field directly, click on the proper tool (button or field), then double-click on the object while holding down the Shift key. A script window with a sample script is shown in Figure 8-2.

Figure 8-2. Script Window and Sample Script

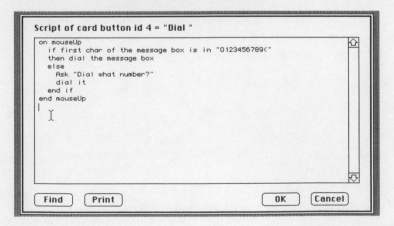

```
Script of card button id 4 = "Dial "

on mouseUp
  if first char of the message box is in "0123456789("
  then dial the message box
  else
    Ask "Dial what number?"
    dial it
  end if
end mouseUp
```

Find   Print   OK   Cancel

Scripts can be edited just like any Macintosh text, using the same cut, copy, and paste techniques. Because the menus don't operate when the script window is opened, you have to edit with the keyboard equivalents—Command-X for cut, Command-C for copy, and Command-V for paste. You can paste text into a script from any source via the Clipboard. This is quite helpful when you are writing a number of scripts with the same basic format; you can store the basic format in the Clipboard and then load it into a new object's script window, ready for customizing. When the script is finished, click OK or press the Enter key. To stop a script in progress, type Command-. (period).

HyperCard provides some powerful script-searching capabilities.

- To look for a term in the current script, click on the Find button (Command-F), and type in the word you want to search for. Then press Return to initiate the search from the current insertion point.
- To find the next occurrence of the specified text, press Command-G (aGain).
- To search for text that you've selected, press Command-H. Pressing Command-H again will also find the next occurrence of the text.
- To select the entire script, press Command-A.
- To print a script, click on the Print button. This will print the entire script or any part of it that you've selected. To stop printing, type Command-. (period).

Script Format

Scripts all follow a certain structure.

- The first line of a script is a trap for a system message, like "on mouseUp" or "on newCard." The word *on* is always the first word of a script.
- Next come the command lines, like "go next card" or "doMenu Recent." You can include up to 32K's worth (that's about 16 to 18 pages) of commands in a script. It's unlikely that you'll ever write a script of that size; most scripts are less than half a page long.

• The contents of control structures are indented.
• All "on" statements and control structures must have an "end" statement to close them. For example, "on mouseUp" is always matched with "end mouseUp." "Repeat three times" must be closed with "end repeat."
• The last line in the script must begin with "end" and must close the event trap at the beginning of the script.

HyperCard automatically sets up an indention system to format your script. Flush left is used for the beginning and ending of the script (on and end statements). The first indention is used for commands. Further indentions are allotted for nested control structures. Every level of indention has to be reversed with an end statement; the script has to end flush left again.

You are not limited to one handler per object. An object's script can have many handlers, each triggered by a different system message. Create a field script with the following three handlers to see what happens:

```
on mouseEnter
    beep 2
end mouseEnter

on mouseWithin
    play "boing"
end mouseWithin

on mouseLeave
    ask "Are You Sure?"
end mouseLeave
```

Each part of the script should be separated by a line space. Look at the Home stack script to get an idea of how multiple handlers are formatted and used.

Scripting Hints

Develop good programming habits as you begin to write your own scripts. One of the best things you can do, for yourself and for anyone who might be reading your scripts, is to add explanatory comments in the script itself. You can do this by typing a double hyphen (--) and then typing your comments. For example:

```
on mouseUp
     go card id 24456        --that's the answer card; copy it with the
                             --the stack
end mouseUp
```

Use a soft return (Option-Return) if your comment takes more than a line.

Watch the indentions of your script. If the script doesn't end flush left, you've got a problem. This is most likely to happen if you are using nested control structures (see the next chapter). And, it's easy to forget to add an ending line like "end if," or "end repeat." Hit the Tab key to try to balance the script's indentions.

Immediately test a script before you do anything else, like copying it for twenty other objects. *HyperCard* won't tell you if there is a syntax or other problem with the script until you try the script out. If there's a problem, you'll see a dialog box like the one in Figure 8-3.

Figure 8-3. Script Error Box

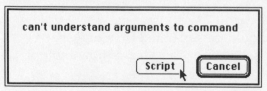

Finally, study other scripts. It's a little like learning to write plays. A playwright draws primarily on his or her own ideas, but also studies the style of other writers, looking to see how they have dealt with common problems of plotting, narrative, and language. The difference with *HyperCard* is that you can simply copy the scripts that other people have written, adding your own modifications. You'll probably learn to write scripts faster by studying existing scripts than by any other method. Try to look for the terms described above, and see how they are linked together. The scripts included on the *HyperCard* disks are the first, and in some ways the best, source of script ideas. You'll also find hundreds of stacks and thousands of scripts in the public domain; you can use these in your own stacks, although you should be careful about redistributing copyrighted material.

Analyzing a Sample Script

The following script (which also appears in Figure 8-2) is for the Dial button on the Phone card. It demonstrates many of the script concepts discussed above. Below, each script line is explained.

```
on mouseUp
    if first char of the message box is in "0123456789("
    then dial the message box
    else
      Ask "Dial what number?"
        dial it
    end if
end mouseUp
```

on mouseUp

Every script must begin with an "on" statement to receive a message sent by *HyperCard* or another object. In this case, the script is primed to receive a message that the mouse button has been released within the perimeter of the button. Once mouseUp is received, the script goes into action.

if first char of the message box is in "0123456789("

This is the first line of an if . . . then . . . else control structure. The statement is testing to see if a phone number has been typed into the message box. The writer of the script has made the assumption that if the first character in the message box is a number or parenthesis—if the first character is one of the characters in the text string "0123456789("—then it must be the first character of a phone number.

then dial the message box
The second part of the if . . . then . . . else structure answers the query raised by the previous line. If the first condition is met—if the message box contains text, and if the first character is a numeral or parenthesis—then the script can dial the phone number using the dial command.

else
This sets up the third part of the if . . . then . . . else control structure. The script is saying, "If the test just proposed didn't work—if there wasn't any text in the message box, for example—then the next lines will describe the action to take."

Ask "Dial what number?"
The ask command creates a dialog box labeled with the text in quotation marks and containing an empty field. The stack user is expected to type into the field the number he or she wants to dial. The number is automatically put into the special local variable, It.

dial it
The number in It is dialed with the dial command. It is then emptied.

end if
Any if . . . then . . . else statement or other control structure has to be closed with an end statement.

end mouseUp
The script is closed with the final end statement.

For More Information

If your appetite for HyperTalk programming has been whetted by this brief introduction, you can obtain more detailed and technical information by contacting the Apple Programmers' and Developers' Association, 290 SW 43rd Street, Renton, Washington 98055, (206) 251-6548. APDA publishes a *Hyper-Card* Script Language guide that covers techniques for more advanced programmers. Another good source of information about HyperTalk is your local Macintosh users' group.

Chapter 9
HyperTalk Dictionary

Chapter 9
HyperTalk Dictionary

This chapter lists every HyperTalk command, constant, control structure, function, operator, property, and system message in alphabetical order according to category. Also included for each term are the parameter format(s), a description of how the term is used, and examples.

Parameter Notation

A standard notation for describing the parameter(s) of a HyperTalk statement has emerged. The basic format is:

term <parameter>

In the following sample,

send <message> to <target>

send is a command, and the words enclosed in arrow brackets are the types of information that must be plugged into the parameter. For example, in the statement **send mouseUp to card button id 4567**, mouseUp is the <message> and **card button id 4567** is the <target>. A word that must appear as itself (like **to** in the sample) is not enclosed by any kind of brackets.

Some parts of a statement are optional. These are enclosed in square brackets, as in:

visual [effect] <effect name> [<speed>] [to black | white]

The only parts of this statement that are essential are the command **visual** and the <effect name> (for example, **zoom open**). Everything within the square brackets modifies the basic statement (except for the word **effect**, which just makes the statement easier to read). When there is a choice among modifiying terms, they are separated by a vertical line, as in **black | white** above.

Examples for most terms can be tested in the message box, except for control structures, system messages, and a few other terms. When a script is used as an example, you can try the script out for yourself by creating an object for the script and modifying the script as necesary. For example, if an example script sends a mouseUp message to an imaginary button named *TRex*, you can modify the script to send a mouseUp message to a real button in the stack you are working with.

Commands

add

Format:

add <source> to <container>

Action:

Adds a number to another number in a container, or adds the number in one container to the number in another container

Examples:

```
add field 1 to field 2    --sums the numbers in field 1 and 2
                          --and puts the sum into field 2
add 10 to it              --adds 10 to the number in it
add 52 + field 1 to card field "Weeks till Bastille Day"
```

Any expression or formula that evaluates to a number can be added to a number in a container.

answer

Format:

answer <question> [with <reply> [or <reply> [or <reply>]]]

Action:

Shows a dialog box requiring an answer from the user

Examples:

```
answer "Ready to Write a Script?" with "Not Yet" or "Go For It!"
answer "Can You Do This from the Message Box?" with "Yes" or "Cancel"
```

Answer works well with if . . . then control structures—for example:

```
if word 1 of field 1 is "no"
then answer "Shall we continue?" with "OK" or "Cancel" or "Go Home"
```

ask

Format:

<question> [with <reply>]

Action:

Displays a dialog box asking for a typed reply and puts the reply into the local variable, It

Examples:

ask "What is your name?
ask "How old are you?" with "I'm   years old."

The part of the parameter after "with" is text that will show in the dialog box.

ask password

Format:

<question> [with <reply>]

Action:

Displays dialog box that asks the user to type in the proper password

Example:

ask password "What's the password"

This password is stored separately from the Protect Stack password. The stack author can craft a stack script so if the password does not match an encrypted version already stored within the program, the user will be denied access to the stack.

beep

Format:

beep [<number of beeps>]

Action:

Makes the specified number of beeps

Examples:

beep
beep 10

choose

Format:

choose <tool name> tool

Action:

Selects a tool in the Tools menu

Examples:

choose field tool

choose bucket tool

choose round rect tool

This is the same as selecting the tools with the pointer.

click

Format:

click at <horizontal coordinate, vertical coordinate> [with <modifier key>[, <modifier key>]]

Action:

Clicks on the specified location

Examples:

click at 50, 150

click at 50, 150 with shiftKey, optionKey

This works like clicking the mouse and pressing a modifier key. You need to have the coordinates of the object you want to click on. Use

get location of <object name>

to find out a valid location for the object.

convert

Format:

convert <container> to <desired format>

Action:

Transforms date and time information to one of the seven format date/time formats:

1. seconds (secs)
2. long date (Sunday, June 2, 1974)
3. short date (6/2/87)
4. abbreviated date (abbr date) (Sun Jun 2, 1974)
5. long time (12-hour clock, 12:01:45 AM, or 24-hour clock, 24:01:45)

6. short time (12:01 AM, 24:01)
7. dateItems (year, month, day, hour, minute, second, and weekday, starting with Sunday, in this form: 1972, 6,2,12,01,45,1)

Examples:

convert field "today's date" to secs	--computes the number of
	--seconds from 12:00AM,
	--January 1, 1904 to the
	--present date and time
convert temptime to the long time	--temptime is a variable
	--containing the short time

Use the convert command to help you add or subtract dates and times. It's easiest to convert dates and times to seconds, add or subtract them, and then convert them back to more familiar formats.

delete

Format:
  delete <item>
Action:
  Eliminates specified text from a field or container
Examples:
  delete word 1 of card field "TRex"
  delete item 4 of it
  delete word 4 to 5 of line 2 of field id 4567

dial

Format:
  dial <phone number> [with [modem] <modem settings>]
Action:
  Dials the specified phone number through a modem or other device
Examples:

dial "569-6939"	--with an acoustic coupler
dial "569-6939" with modem "ATDT"	
dial selection with "ATDT"	--dials the selected number

divide

Format:

divide <container> by <source>

Action:

Divides the number in a container by the source number, which can be a number in another container

Examples:

```
divide field 1 by 3              --divides the number in field 1 by 3
divide field 1 by field 5        --puts the quotient into field 5
divide total 1 + total 2 by total 3   --these are local variables
```

do

Format:

do <source>

Action:

Executes a command or the first line of a script in a container

Example:

```
on mouseUp
    put "go home" into field 1
    do field 1
end mouseUp
```

The text in field 1, *go home,* is treated as a command by do. The script will take you home. You can enter any command into a container (usually a field) and use do to run the command.

doMenu

Format:

doMenu <menu option>

Action:

Makes a menu choice

Examples:

```
doMenu "Print Card"
doMenu "Copy Button"
doMenu "Field Info..."
```

Any menu option can be called with doMenu. Make sure that the option is specified *exactly* as it appears in the menu.

drag

Format:

drag from <location> to <location> [with <modifier key>[, <modifier key>]]

Action:

Mimics dragging with the mouse and any modifier keys

Examples:

choose line tool
set linesize to 4
drag from 50,150 to 100,150
drag from 100,150 to 100,50
drag from 100,50 to 50,50
drag from 50,50 to 50,150

Try the above commands from the message box. *HyperCard* will draw a rectangle in the upper left portion of the screen. You can do any kind of drawing (except freehand drawing) with drag.

edit script

Format:

edit script of <target>

Action:

Shows you the script window for the target object

Examples:

edit script of button "home"
edit script of stack "home"

Use this only if you want users to edit the scripts of your objects.

find

Format:

find [char[acter]s | word] <source> [in <field>]

Action:

Performs a text search in the current stack or in a specified field

Examples:
find "the"
find chars "the" in field 1
find word "the"

If you just want to search a stack for a specific word, use Find from the message box.

flash

Format:
flash<number of times>
Action:
creates a flashing visual effect over the whole screen
Example:
flash 4

get

Format:
get <expression>
get <property> [of <target>]
Action:
Puts an expression or its value into It, the local variable; also gets the properties of objects
Examples:
get the time
get word 2 of field "TRex"

Functionally, getting an expression is the same as putting the expression into the local variable, It.
get textStyle of card field id 7654
get location of button "Home"
get script of card 3

Get puts the property of the target object into the local variable It.

global

Format:
global <variable name(s)>
Action:
Creates a global variable with the specified name(s)

178

Examples:
global TRex
global temp1, temp2, temp3 --creates 3 globals

Although the content of a global variable won't change until you want it to, you must declare the global in a message handler before you use it. Add the statement *global TRex* in the message handler before you use the content of global TRex. Use the put command to store material in a global.

go
Format:
go [to] <destination>
Action:
Takes you from card to card and stack to stack
Examples:
go home
go to last card --of this stack
go to stack "Area Codes"

help
Format:
help
Action:
Takes you to the Help stacks
Example:
help

hide
Format:
hide menubar I <window> I <field> or <button>
Action:
Makes the specified object disappear
Examples:
hide menubar
hide bkgnd button id 3456
hide message

Use the hide command in conjunction with the show command (see below). It's good form to show the menu bar or the message box again when a stack is closed.

multiply

Format:

multiply <container> by <source>

Action:

Gives the product of the number in the container times another number or a number in another container

Examples:

multiply field 1 by 3	--triples the number in field 1
multiply field 1 by field 5	--puts the product into field 5
multiply total 1 + total 2 by total 3	--these are local variables

open

Format:

open [<document> with] <application>

Action:

Starts another application and document from *HyperCard*

Examples:

open "FullPaint"
open "Novel" with "MacWrite"
open "HD20:Pictures:TRex" with "HD20:GraphicsApps:MacPaint"

Be sure to give the full pathname of the application and file you want to open. Also, you must give the *exact* name of the application. Sometimes the name of an application will include a version number and/or trademark character.

open file/close file

Format:

open file <file name>
close file <file name>

Action:

Opens an external text file for reading or writing and closes it afterward

Examples:

open file "Q&E:Chap 9"
close file "Q&E:Chap 9"

Be sure to specify the complete pathname of the file you are accessing.

open printing/print/close printing

Format:

open printing [with dialog]
print [all <number> cards] l [this <card>]
close printing

Action:

Controls printing of any group of cards in the order you specify

Example:

```
on mouseUp
    open printing with dialog
    print card 1
    print card 6
    print card id 4321
    print next card
    close printing
end mouseUp
```

This button script sets up a printing task. First it shows you the Print Stack . . . dialog box; then it prints the cards specified. "Close printing" shuts down the printing task. You can also work the print commands through the message box. Type in *open printing with dialog*, then go to the cards you want to print and type in *print this card*.

play

Format:

play <voice> [tempo <speed>] [<notes>] [# (sharp) l b (flat)] [octave] [duration]

Action:

Plays digitized sounds at specified tempo, notes, pitch, octave, and duration. There are four sounds in *HyperCard*'s resources: boing, dialing tones, harpsichord, and silence.

Tempo is a number, with the default value set at 200.

Notes are specified by the letters *a, b, c, d, e, f,* and *g,* as in the musical scale; they can be sharp or flat. You can also use note numbers. Middle C is 60. Use r for rests.

The first note in the parameter should have an octave

number attached; octaves 3, 4, and 5 correspond to the middle octaves on a piano, and sound the best. Any notes in the parameter will be in the same octave until you change the octave by putting in a new octave number.

Notes can be a whole note to a 64th note in duration. Whole notes are designated by *w*, half notes by *h*, quarters by *q*, eighths by *e*, sixteenths by *s*, and thirty-seconds by *t*, and sixty-fourths by *x*.

Examples:
play "boing"
play "harpsichord" tempo 400 "c3w"
play "boing" tempo 200 "at3 b c dw e f gq aw4 b c dt e f gw"

pop

Format:
pop card [into <container>]
Action:
Retrieves last card marked with the push command
Examples:
pop card
pop card into cardHolder --cardHolder is a container

print

Format:
print <file name> with <application>
Action:
Lets you print a file made with another application
Examples:
print "Q&E" with "WriteNow™" --use the exact name of the
                              --application
print "Writings:Rambles" with "MacWrite"
print "Pix:Starfire" with "GraphicsApps:MacPaint"

The print command closes *HyperCard*, opens the application, prints the file, quits the application, and returns you to *HyperCard* at the place from which you exited. It differs from the open printing/print/close printing commands, which act only on cards.

push

Format:

push [this I recent] card

Action:

Earmarks a card for later retrieval using the pop command

Examples:

push this card
push recent card

put

Format:

put <source> [into I before I after I <container>]

Action:

Takes information from one source or container and moves it to another container

Examples:

put the long date   --puts the date into the message box
put field 1 + field 2 into field 3
put 5 into it
put it into field "Add 5"
put " TRex " before word 1 of card field id 5656

Use into, before, and after to put text or numbers into a text string. If the text in field id 5656 is "was a theropod," then putting "TRex" before word 1 of the field will change the text to "TRex was a theropod." Putting "TRex" *into* word 1 of the field would yield "TRex a theropod" ("TRex" is substituted for "was"). Putting "TRex" *after* word 1 of the field would give you "was TRex a theropod."

read

Format:

read from file <filename> until <delimiting character> I <number of bytes>

Action:

Reads text from an external text file and puts it into *HyperCard* fields. You must open the external file with the open command and close it afterward with the close command.

Examples:

read from file "Writings:MyStory" until return
read from file "Ramblings" for 100   --100 bytes

183

reset paint

Format:

reset paint

Action:

Sets all the paint tools and menu options to their default values

Example:

reset paint

send

Format:

send <message> to <target>

Action:

Issues a message to any specified object (the target)

Examples:

send "mouseUp" to bkgnd button "next"

send "mouseUp" to bkgnd button id 5677

send "tabKey" to bkgnd field "Subtotal"

Most messages sent with send are system messages.

set

Format:

set <property> [of <target>] to <desired setting>

Action:

Changes the property of an object to a desired setting

Examples:

set textFont of field 1 to "Chicago"

set location of field 1 to 100,200

Set autohilite of bkgnd button "Home" to false--switches off the auto-hilite
                                    --feature if it is on

show

Format:

show menubar | <window> | <field or button> [at <location>]

show [<number> | all] cards

Action:

Reveals at a desired location any screen object that may have been hidden; also shows specified number of cards belonging to the current stack

Examples:

```
show menubar
show tool window at 100,100
show message at 100,200
show all cards          --in the stack
show 4 cards            --the next four cards
```

Use the show command in conjunction with the hide command (see above).

sort

Format:

sort [ascending I descending] [text I numeric I international I dateTime] by <container>

Action:

Puts cards into an order according to the item specified in the container

Examples:

```
sort by last word of first line of field 1
sort descending numeric by field "Total Population"
sort ascending dateTime by field "Admitted to the United Nations"
```

Using the text parameter sorts by the ASCII value of the character. Numeric sort sorts by number value. International sort looks for non-English ligatures and diacritical marks and sorts them into proper order. DateTime sorts by any valid date and time format, like 12/25/87 (as long as the date is after January 1, 1904).

subtract

Format:

subtract <source> from <container>

Action:

Subtracts a number from a number in a container, or subtracts the number in one container from the number in another

Examples:
```
on mouseUp
    get loc of field 1
    click at it
    type "Here I am! Watch me type! Goodbye..."
andmouseUp
```
Any expression or formula that evaluates to a number can be subtracted from a number in a container.

type
Format:
type <source>
Action:
Types text into a container, usually a field
Examples:
```
type "Miriam"
type "Less" & return & "Is more"
```
Type only operates from a script, not the message box. In the script, first select the field to receive the text by clicking at it with the "click" command.

visual
Format:
visual [effect] <type of effect> [<speed>] [to black | white]
Action:
Creates a cinematic transition from one card to the next. These are the visual effects available:

barn door open | close
dissolve checkerboard | venetian blinds
iris open | close
scroll right | left | up | down
wipe right | left | up | down
zoom open | in | close | out

Four speeds are available: very slow, slow, normal, and fast.
Examples:
```
visual effect zoom open
visual barn door close fast to black
visual wipe left to white
```

Put the visual command statement before the go command statement that actually takes you to the next card. Note that visual doesn't operate from the message box.

wait/wait until/wait while

Format:

> wait [for] <length of time> ticks | seconds
>> wait until <true or false statement>
>> wait while <true of false statement>

Action:

Makes the script wait for a specified time, until an event occurs, or until a function returns true or false

Examples:

```
wait 2 secs
wait until arrowKey up
wait while mouseDown
wait for it        --waits for the value of it
```

The wait commands also will not work from the message box.

write

Format:

> write <source> to file <file name>

Action: Writes *HyperCard* text to an external text file. You must open the external file with the open command and close it afterward with the close command.

Examples:

```
write field 1 to file "HyperCardInfo"
write field 2 to file "Sales:SpreadsheetData"
write tab to file "Sales:SpreadSheetData"        --you must write your own
                                                 --delimiter
```

Constants

Constants are terms that substitute for a predefined value. HyperTalk constants can be used to enter values from the mouse and keyboard, such as down, quote, and tab, or to show whether certain values are true or false.

down

Action:

Returns a down value for a key or the mouse button

Examples:

if the shiftKey is down then beep
if the mouse is down then beep2

empty

Action:

Returns the null or empty value

Examples:

put empty into field 1
if field 1 is empty then ask "Where's Text?"

false

Examples:

set temp to false --puts false into the variable temp
if temp is false then doMenu "New Card"

formFeed

Action:

Returns ASCII value 12 (move paper to top of next page) for sending to printer

Example:

write formfeed to file "Rambles"

lineFeed

Action:

Returns ASCII value 10 (move cursor or paper to next line) for sending to terminal or printer

Example:

write lineFeed to file "Rambles"

quote

Action:

Lets you include quotation marks in a text string

Example:

put quote & "What fools these mortals be!" & quote into field 1

return

Action:

Lets you include the equivalent of a Return keypress in a script

Examples:

put return after word 4 of line 2 of field 1
read from file "Rambles" until return

space

Action:

Lets you include the equivalent of a spacebar keypress in a script

Examples:

put space after word 2 of field 1
write to file "Poem" until space & space & space

tab

Action:

Lets you include the equivalent of a Tab keypress in a script

Examples:

read from file "Rambles" until tab
put tab after word 1 of field 2

true

Examples:

set temp2 to true   --puts true into the variable temp2
if temp2 is true then doMenu "New Card"

up

Action:

Lets you put the key or mouse button-up value into a script

Examples:

if the mouse is up then beep
repeat until tabKey is up

zero through ten

Action:

Lets you use the words zero through ten in a script as though they were numerals

Example:

if field is five then beep

Control Structures

Control structures cannot be operated from the message box;
you must test them in an actual script.

exit

Format:

   exit if

   exit repeat

   exit <current message handler>

Action:

   Takes you out of an if . . . then structure, repeat loop, or
   message handler

Example:

```
on mouse Up
    put "2=2" into msg box
    repeat 10
        if the value of the msg is true then
            beep 2
            exit repeat
        else play "boing"
    end repeat
end mouseUp
```

if . . . then

Format:

   if <true or false expression>

   then <command>

   end if

Action:

   Tests for the truth or falsity of an expression and takes action based on the result of the test

Example:

```
if "a spade" is "a spade"
then
    beep 3
endif
```

if . . . then . . . else

Format:

   if <true or false expression>

   then <command>

   else <command>

   end if

191

Action:

Tests for the truth or falsity of an expression and takes a "then" action based on a true result or an "else" action based on a false result

Example:
```
if "black" is "white"
then
    beep 2
else play "boing"
endif
```

next repeat

Format:

next repeat

Action:

Provides a way to shorten a repeat loop if a condition is met

Example:
```
repeat until the mouse is up
    add score to field 1   --score is a local variable
    if field 1 < 50
    then
        next repeat
    else beep 2
end repeat
```

pass

Format:

pass <message>

Action:

Allows you to pass trapped messages on up the hierarchy. Use pass when you want to trap certain forms of a message but not others.

Example:
```
on doMenu snooper
    if snooper is "Find..." then
        ask "Search this way instead"
        find it
    end if
    pass doMenu
end doMenu
```

repeat
repeat until
repeat while
repeat with

Format:

> repeat [for] <number of repeats> [times]
> repeat until <true or false expression>
> repeat while <true or false expression>
> repeat with <variable> = <low number> to <high number>
> repeat with <variable> = <high number> down to <low
> number>

Action:

> Repeats a command or set of commands for a specified
> number of times, until certain conditions are met, while an-
> other action is going on, or until a bound is reached

Examples:

```
on mouseUp
   repeat for 5 times
      beep 2
      wait 30
   end repeat
end mouseUp

on mouseUp
   repeat until the mouse is down
      beep 2
      wait 30
   end repeat
end mouseUp

on mouseDown
   repeat while the mouse is down
      beep 2
      wait 30
   end repeat
end mouseDown

on startUp
   repeat with i = 1 to the number of bkgnd fields
                     --i is the variable, the bounds are 1
                     --and the number of fields in the bkgnd

      put stackUpdate into field i
                     --puts the contents of the container
                     --stackUpdate into every field in the
```

```
                        --bkgnd, starting with the first field
                        --and repeating with each field up to the
                        --number of fields in the bkgnd
        end repeat
    end startUp
```

Repeat with structures provides a convenient way to make changes to a number of similar objects at once, including scripts.

Functions

Functions return results. Typing

sqrt of 256   --square root

into the message box returns the answer, 16. Functions also require *arguments*, which you can think of as being like parameters. In the statement above, "of 256" is the argument. Arguments can be written in two formats

the time
time ( )
the random of 1000
random (1000)

with the function preceded by **the** and the argument following **of**, or with the argument in parentheses. (Even if there is no value for the argument, the second format requires parentheses.)

You can use the name of the function to stand in for the value it represents in any script.

the abs
Format:
   the abs of <number>
Action:
   Returns a number's absolute value
Examples:
   the abs of −50
   abs (−1)
   abs (50)

the annuity
Format:
   the annuity of <periodic rate, number of periods>

Action:

Returns the present value of an annuity payment
The formula is:

$$\text{annuity of rate, number} = \frac{1-(1 + r)^{(-n)}}{r}$$

Examples:

the annuity of 0.15, 24
annuity (0.15, 24)

Multiply the result by the amount of a payment to get the present value of the payments on an annuity.

the atan

Format:

the atan of <angle in radians>

Action:

Returns the arctangent of the specified angle

Examples:

the atan of 45
atan (45)

the average

Format:

the average of <number list>

Action:

Returns the mean average of numbers in a list. The numbers must be separated by commas.

Examples:

the average of 10, 20, 30, 40, 50,
average (1, 2, 3, 4, 5)

the charToNum

Format:

the charToNum of <character>

Action:

Returns the ASCII number of a character. Every keyboard character has an ASCII number; lowercase letters have an ASCII value exactly 32 less than the uppercase version of the same letter. CharToNum reverses the action of numToChar (see below).

Examples:

the charToNum of "A"
the charToNum of "a"
the charToNum of "&"

the clickLoc

Action:

Returns the coordinates of the previous mouse click. This can be used instead of mouseLoc (see below) if the user may have had time to move the mouse while the script was running.

Examples:

the clickLoc
put the clickLoc into field 1
if item 1 of the clickLoc < 50 then answer "Move to the Right"

the commandKey

Action:

Returns whether the Command key is up or down. Use this to test whether the key is being pressed.

Examples:

if commandKey is down then answer "Your wish is my Command"

the compound

Format:

the compound of <periodic rate, number of periods>

Action:

Returns the future value of a periodic payment.
The formula is:

$$\text{compound of rate, number} = (1+r)^n$$

Examples:

the compound of 0.15, 24
compound (0.15, 24)

Multiply the result by the periodic payment to get the future value of the investment.

the cos

Format:
the cos of <angle in radians>
Action:
Returns the cosine of an angle
Examples:
the cos of 60
cos (60)

the date
the long date
the abbreviated/abbrev/abbr date

Action:
Returns today's date. The date returns the format

12/1/88

The long date returns the format

Monday, December 1, 1988

The abbreviated date returns the format

Mon, Dec 1, 1988

Examples:
the long date
put the date into field 1
put word 2 of item 2 of the long date into field 2   --puts in the day

the diskSpace

Format:
the diskSpace
Action: Returns the unused space on the current disk in bytes.
Example:
the diskSpace

the exp
the exp1
the exp2

Format:

the exp of <number>

the exp1 of <number>

the exp2 of <number>

Action:

Exp returns the natural (base-e) exponent; exp1 returns the natural exponent less 1; exp2 returns the base-2 exponent

Examples:

the exp of 5

exp (5)

exp1 (5)

exp2 (5)

the length

Format:

the length of <container>

Action:

Returns the number of characters in a text string in a container

Examples:

the length of field 1

the length of the msg box

the ln
the ln1

Format:

the ln of <number>

the ln1 of <number>

Action:

Ln returns the natural log of a number; ln1 returns the natural log of 1 plus the number

Examples:

the ln of 5

ln (5)

ln1 (5)

the max

Format:
the max of <list of numbers>

Action:
Returns the highest number in a list

Examples:
the max of 10, 40, 20, 30, 80, 2, 3, 68
max (10, 40, 20, 30, 80, 2, 3, 68)

the min

Format:
the min of <list of numbers>

Action:
Returns the lowest number in a list

Examples:
the min of 110, 20, 30, 45, 43, 2, 89
min (110, 20, 30, 45, 43, 2, 89)

the mouse

Action:
Returns whether the mouse button is up or down. Use this to test for when the mouse button is being pressed.

Examples:
the mouse
if the mouse is up
then
    put "Please click" into the message box
endif

the mouseClick

Action:
Returns *true* if the button has been clicked, *false* if it hasn't. Use the mouseClick to test for whether the user has clicked the mouse button.

Example:
the mouseClick

the mouseH
Action:
> Returns the horizontal coordinates of the cursor active spot.
> Use mouseH to precisely locate the cursor active spot along
> the *x*-axis of the screen.

Examples:
the mouseH
put the mouseH into field 1

the mouseLoc
Action:
> Returns the horizontal and vertical coordinates of the cursor
> active spot. Use mouseLoc to determine the exact location of
> the cursor active spot on the screen.

Examples:
the mouseLoc --returns coordinates in format (h, v)
show message at the mouseLoc

the mouseV
Action:
> Returns the vertical coordinate of the cursor active spot

Examples:
the mouseV
get the mouseV
multiply it by 1.5

the number
Format:
> the number [of] <components> in <container>
> the number of backgrounds I cards I buttons I fields

Action:
> Returns the total number of components in a container, or
> the number of cards, buttons, or fields in the current card or
> background, and the number of cards or backgrounds in the
> current stack

Examples:
the number of words in the message box
the number of chars in the message box
the number of cards
the number of bkgnd buttons
the number of bkgnds

the numToChar

Format:
the numToChar of <ASCII value>
Action:
Returns the character of an ASCII value (any number between 0 and 255). NumToChar reverses the action of charToNum.
Examples:
the numToChar of 65
the numToChar of 97
the numToChar of 38

offset

Format:
offset (<expression>, <expression>)
Action:
Returns the number of the character that a word begins with, or the position of an individual character, in a text string.
Examples:
Create a card field "Lincoln" with the text: "the better angels of our nature" in it. Then type into the message box:
offset ("angels", card field "Lincoln")
offset ("g", card field "Lincoln")

the optionKey

Action:
Returns whether the Option key is up or down. Use this to test whether the key is being pressed.
Examples:
if the optionKey is down then answer "What's your option?"

the param
the paramcount
the params

Format:

the param of

the params

the paramcount

Action:

The param returns the text of the specified parameter of the
current message; the params returns all the parameters of
the current message, including the command word; the
paramcount returns the number of parameters in the current
message. The param, the params, and the paramcount are
useful when you want to retrieve part or all of the parameters of a message for use in another script.

Examples:

```
get param(1)        --the first word after the command
get the paramcount
subtract item 3 from it
put the params into temp1
```

the random

Format:

the random of <upper limit>

Action:

Returns a random number between 1 and the upper limit
(not more than 32767)

Examples:

```
the random of 3        --repeat this a few times
the random of 1000
if the random of 6 is 6 then put "It's a match!" into the message box
```

the result

Action:

Returns an error message if a Find or Go command has
failed

Examples:

```
the result
go card 9000
the result
```

the round

Format:
the round of <number>
Action:
Rounds the number to the nearest integer
Examples:
the round of 12.48999
round (99.50010)

the seconds
the secs

Action:
Returns the number of seconds since 12:00 AM, January 1, 1904
Examples:
the secs
put the secs into field 1

the shiftKey

Action:
Returns whether the Shift key is up or down. Use this to test whether the key is being pressed.
Example:
if the shiftKey is down then answer "Shift into overdrive?"

the sin

Format:
the sin of <angle in radians>
Action:
Returns the sine of the angle
Examples:
the sin of 30
sin (90)

the sound

Action:
Returns the name of a sound that is playing, and "done" when the sound is finished

Examples:
beep 50
the sound

Use the sound to trap for the continued playing of a sound that you don't want to interfere with by accessing the disk or proceeding with the script. You won't be able to test this from the message box.

the sqrt

Format:
the sqrt of <number>

Action:
Returns the square root of the number

Examples:
the sqrt of 1521
sqrt (225)

the stackSpace

Format:
the stackSpace

Action:
Returns the size of the current stack in bytes.

Example:
the stackSpace

the tan

Format:
the tan of <angle in radians>

Action:
Returns the tangent of the angle

Examples:
the tan of 70
tan (275)

the target

Action:

Returns the id of the object that was the recipient of the most recent message

Examples:

the target   --from the message box, this is always the current card
put the name of the target into the message box

the ticks

Action:

Returns the number of ticks (jiffies, or 1/60ths of a second) since you last turned on the Mac. The ticks are not an absolute measure of duration and should not be used for very accurate timing of times longer than a few seconds. Use the secs instead.

Examples:

the ticks
put the ticks into field 1
multiply value of field 1 by the ticks

the time
the long time

Action:

Returns the exact time. The time returns the format

    12:01 PM

The long time returns the format

    12:01:30 PM

You can select 12- or 24-hour time from the Control Panel.

Examples:

the time
put the long time into field 1

the tool

Action:

Returns the current tool

Examples:

the tool
if the tool is "rect" then doMenu "opaque"

the trunc

Format:

the trunc of <number>

Action:

Returns the nearest whole number before the specified
number

Examples:

the trunc of 2.99
trunc (10.478)

the value

Format:

the value of <container or expression>

Action:

Calculates the value of an arithmetic expression and returns
the answer

Examples:

Create 2 fields: type 2 + 3 into field 1 and 2 * 3 into field 2.
the value of field 1
the value of field 2
the value of field 1 + field 2

Custom Functions

You can define your own functions using this format:

```
function <function name> [parameter]
    <command>
    return <value>
end <function name>
```

You must call custom functions with the parentheses form, as in:

```
<function name>(<argument>)
```

Operators
+ (plus)
— (minus)
* (multiply)
/ (divide)

Action:
Returns the result of the arithmetic operation

Examples:
```
12+15
1122−456−11
33*17
33/17
```

= (equals)
is
< >, ≠ (is not equal to)
is not

Action:
Compares two expressions or containers and returns true or false

Examples:
```
2=2
2< >2
if field 1< >field 2 then put field 1 into message box
field 1 is field 2
field 2 is not field 3
```

> (greater than)
< (less than)
>= (greater than or equal to)
<= (less than or equal to)

Action:
Compares two expressions or containers and returns true or false

Examples:
```
3<2
3<=4
if field 1> field 2 then subtract 1 from field 1
```

^ (exponent)

Format:

<number or container>^<power>

Action:

Returns the number or container raised to a power

Examples:

3^2	--returns 9
12^3	
total^2	--total is a local variable
field 1^field 2	--the number in field 1 raised to the power of the
	--number in field 2

& (concatenate)
&& (concatenate with space)

Action:

Returns the result of putting together two or more pieces of text, with or without spaces between the text items

Examples:

put"TRex" & "theropod" into field 1
       --returns "TRextheropod"

put "TRex," && "theropod" into field 2
       --returns "TRex theropod"

put field 2 && the long date into message box

and

Format:

<true or false expression> and <true or false expression>

Action:

Returns whether the two expressions taken together are true or false. Both expressions must be true to return true.

Examples:

3>2 and 2>3
if "true" is "false" and "black" is "white", then beep
if "3" is "3" and "green" is "green", then beep

contains
is in
Format:

    \<text1\> contains \<text2\>

    \<text1\> is in \<text2\>

Action:

    Contains returns true or false as to whether text1 includes text2; is in returns true or false as to whether text2 includes text1

Examples:

    "TRex" contains "ex"   --returns true

    "TRex" is in "TRex, theropod"

    field 1 is in field 2

    if "man" is in "woman" then beep 2

div (divide and truncate)
Action:

    Returns the division of one number by another as an integer with no remainder

Examples:

    12 div 5   --returns 2

    144 div 11   --returns 13

mod (modulo)
Action:

    Returns the remainder after one number is divided by another

Examples:

    12 mod 5   --returns 2

    144 mod 11   --returns 1

not
Format:

    not \<true or false expression\>

Action:

    Returns the converse of whether the expression is true or false

211

Examples:
 not (2=2)   --returns false
 not ("a spade" is "a spade")
 if not (3=3) is false then beep

or

Format:
 <true or false expression> or <true or false expression>
Action:
 Returns true if at least one of the expressions is true
Examples:
 "seeing" is "believing" or "green" is "green"   --returns true
 4=5 or 5=4
 if field 1 is true or field 2 is false then beep

--

Format:
 --<comment>
Action:
 HyperTalk ignores any text after double hyphens
Example:
 go card 5 --the answer card

Properties

Most properties are used in conjunction with the get or set commands in the following way:

get the <property>
set the <property> to <true | false> | <property number | name>

You can think of the property as being *on* when it is *true*, and being *off* when it is *false*. It's easy to test most properties from the message box with an appropriate object. Remember that the get command puts the property into the local variable It.

Global properties (those that belong to *HyperCard* itself) include: blindTyping, cursor, dragSpeed, editBkgnd, language, lockScreen, numberFormat, powerKeys, and userLevel.

Window properties (the message box and Tools and Patterns palettes are windows) include: loc(ation), rect(angle), and visible.

Painting properties include: brush, centered, filled, grid, lineSize, multiple, multiSpace, pattern, polySides, textAlign, textFont, textHeight, textSize, and textStyle.

Stack properties include freeSize, name, script, and size.

Background properties include name, and script.

Card properties include id, name, number, and script.

Field properties include: id, loc(ation), lockText, name, rect(angle), script, scroll, showLines, style, textAlign, textFont, textHeight, textSize, textStyle, visible, and wideMargins.

Button properties include: autoHilite, hilite, icon, loc(ation), name, rect(angle), script, showName, style, textAlign, textFont, textHeight, textSize, textStyle, and visible.

autoHilite

Format:

autoHilite <true I false>

Action:

Governs button auto highlighting (except radio buttons and check boxes)

Examples:

get autoHilite of button "Home"
set autoHilite of button "Home" to true

blindTyping

Format:

blindTyping <true I false>

Action:

Governs whether you can type commands to the message box when it is hidden

Example:

get the blindTyping

brush

Format:

brush <1 to 32>

Action:

Governs what brush is selected from the Brush Shape dialog box.

There are 32 brushes, numbered 1 to 32 starting with the top left and working down the columns. The default brush is number 8.

Examples:

set brush to 1   --the large square
set brush to 13   --the long vertical line

centered

Format:
centered <true | false>

Action:
Governs Draw Centered in the Options menu.

Examples:
get the centered
set the centered to true

cursor

Format:
cursor <id or name>

Action:
Sets which cursor wil be displayed. Four cursors are available: *I*-beam (1), crosshairs (2), Maltese cross (3), and the wristwatch (4).

Example:
set cursor to 1

You cannot "get" the cursor setting. The cursor will return to its previous setting when the script is finished.

dragSpeed

Format:
dragSpeed <number>

Action:
Governs the drag speed. The fastest drag speed is 0; otherwise, drag speed is measured in pixels per second, with low numbers being slower than high numbers.

Examples:
get dragSpeed
set dragSpeed to 0
set dragSpeed to 150

editBkgnd

Format:
   editBkgnd <true | false>
Action:
   Governs whether you are editing in the background or card
   domain.
Examples:
   set editBkgnd to true   --puts you into the bkgnd domain
   set editBkgnd to false   --puts you into the card domain

filled

Format:
   filled <true | false>
Action:
   Governs the Draw Filled option in the Options menu
Examples:
   get the filled
   set the filled to false

freeSize

Format:
   freeSize
Action:
   Tells the free size of a stack in bytes
Example:
   freeSize of stack "Home"
You can't set the freeSize of a stack.

grid

Format:
   grid <true | false>
Action:
   Governs the Grid option in the Options menu
Examples:
   get the grid
   set the grid to true

hilite

Format:
hilite <true | false>
Action:
Governs highlighting of radio buttons and check boxes
Examples:
get hilite of button "Browsing"   --on User Prefs card
set hilite to false   --radio button won't hilite when clicked on

icon

Format:
icon <number | name>
Action:
Governs icon of button
Examples:
get icon of button "Home"
set icon of button id 23 to "Sort"
set icon of button id 23 to 2002

id

Format:
id
Action:
Tells the id number of the specified object
Example:
get id of button "Home"
id of this card

You can't set the id of an object.

language

Format:
language <language name>
Action:
Governs operation of the language translator. Some versions of *HyperCard* have built-in foreign language translators that translates English scripts into the language checked on the

User Preferences card. The language property lets you set the language from a script.

Example:

set language to French

lineSize

Format:

lineSize <1 to 8>

Action:

Governs the drawing line width in pixels. There are six widths: 1, 2, 3, 4, 5 or 6, 7 or 8. The default size is 1.

Examples:

get the lineSize
set the lineSize to 4

loc

Format:

loc[ation]

Action:

Governs the location of the upper left corner of a window, field, or button.

Examples:

get the loc of the message box
get the loc of tool window
set loc of button "home" to 200, 200:

lockMessages

Format:

lockMessages <true | false>

Action:

Governs what messages will be allowed to pass while a script is running

Examples:

set lockMessages to true
set lockMessages to false

Set lockMessages to true to prevent any automatic messages (like openCard and newCard) from being passed except for the ones generated by the current handler. LockMessages will always reset itself to false at the end of a script, but you can do it earlier if the script calls for it.

lockRecent

Format:
lockRecent <true | false>
Action:
Governs whether cards will be posted to the Recent card
Examples:
set lockRecent to true
set lockRecent to false

lockScreen

Format:
lockScreen <true | false>
Action:
Governs what screens will be shown while a script is running
Examples:
set lockscreen to true
set lockscreen to false

Set lockScreen to true to keep a desired screen visible even though the script is going to and from other cards. LockScreen will always reset itself to false at the end of a script, but you can do it earlier if the script calls for it.

lockText

Format:
lockText <true | false>
Action:
Governs the locking of text in a field
Examples:
get lockText
set lockText of bkgnd field 2 to true   --locks the text in the field

multiple

Format:

multiple <true I false>

Action:

Governs Draw Multiple in the Options menu

Examples:

get the multiple
set the multiple to true

multiSpace

Format:

multiSpace <1 to 9>

Action:

Governs the spacing between multiples
The numbers 1 through 9 refer to the number of pixels
separating multiple images made with the Draw Multiple
feature.

Examples:

get the multiSpace
set the multiSpace to 6

name

Format:

[short I long] name of <object>

Action:

Governs the name of any object. There are several name
formats that are returned by invoking the name property.
The default name format for a bkgnd field named *Total* on a
card named *May Expenses* in a stack with the pathname *Financial Stacks:Expenses 88* is

card field "Total"

The short name returns

Total

The long name returns

card field "Total" of Card "May Expenses" of stack
"Financial Stacks:Expenses 88"

Examples:
name of this background   --shows the name in the message box
get the name of this stack   --gets the name of the current stack
get the long name of this stack
get the name of field 1
set the name of card button "Home" to "House"

numberFormat

Format:
numberFormat \<format\>
Action:
Governs the way numbers are displayed. Typical number formats are
"0.00" (dollars and cents)
"0." (whole numbers only)
"0.########" (fractional precision to 8 places, with no trailing zeros). You can have any number of crosshatches for any desired degree of precision.
Examples:
set numberFormat to "0.00"
set numberFormat to "0.#######################"

pattern

Format:
pattern \<1 to 40\>
Action:
Governs what pattern is currently active. Each pattern in the Pattern palette has a number, starting with 1 at the upper left and working down the columns.
Examples:
get the pattern
set the pattern to 37   --the trellis

polySides

Format:
polySides \<any number over 2\>

Action:

Governs the number of sides of the regular polygon tool. This lets you set more kinds of regular polygons than are available from the Polygon Sides dialog box.

Examples:

```
get polySides
set polysides to 9        --a nonagon
set polySides to 100      --a near-circle
```

powerKeys

Format:

powerKeys <true I false>

Action:

Governs whether the power keys are active or inactive

Examples:

```
set powerKeys to false    --if you don't want the user to have
                          --access to the power keys
```

This is usually set from the User Preferences card.

rect

Format:

rect[angle]

Action:

Gives upper left and lower right coordinates of a window, field, or button

Example:

```
get the rect of msg
```

The rect property cannot be set.

script

Format:

script of <object>

Action:

Lets you manage a script from another script. You can start, stop, and modify any script from another script by getting and setting the target script.

Examples:

get the script of this card   --puts the script into it
put "go to next card" & return into line 1 of it   --changes a line in the
    --script

get the script of button "Sort"
set the script of button "Sort" to newScript   --replaces the script
    --with a new script in
    --the container newScript

scroll

Format:

scroll <pixels>

Action:

Governs scrolling of a scrolling field in pixels from the top of the field. Lets you scroll the text in a scrolling field automatically or save the scroll position so the text will go back to that scroll position later.

Examples:

get the scroll of card field 2
set the scroll of card field 2 to 32   --shows text two
    --16-point lines down

showLines

Format:

showLines <true | false>

Action:

Governs whether a field shows lines

Examples:

get showLines
set showLines of field 2 to true   --shows lines in field

showName

Format:

showName <true | false>

Action:

Governs the showName button feature

Examples:

get the showName of button "Home"
set the showName of button "Home" to true

size

Format:
size

Action:
Tells size of stack in bytes

Example:
get size stack "Home"

You can't set the stack size.

style

Format:
style <style type>

Action:
Governs style of buttons and fields. Field styles include opaque, rect(angle), scrolling, shadow, and transparent. Button styles include checkBox, opaque, radioButton, rect(angle), roundRect, shadow, and transparent.

Examples:
get style of field 1
get style of button "Home"
set style of field 1 to scrolling
set style of button "Home" to shadow

textAlign

Format:
textAlign <left | right | center>

Action:
Governs alignment of text in a button, a field, or in graphic text

Examples:
get textAlign
set textAlign to right

textFont

Format:
textFont <font name>

Action:
Governs font of text in a button, a field, or in graphic text

Examples:
get textFont
set textFont to Chicago

textHeight

Format:
textHeight <leading>
Action:
Governs points between lines of text (leading) in a button, a field, or in graphic text
Examples:
get textHeight
set textHeight to 18   --points

textSize

Format:
textSize <font size>
Action:
Governs point size of text in a button, a field, or in graphic text
Examples:
get textSize
set textSize to 14   --points

textStyle

Format:
textStyle <style type[, style type]>
Action:
Governs text style of text in a button, a field, or in graphic text. Available styles are plain, bold, italic, underline, outline, shadow, condense, and extend. You can combine these styles however you like (except with plain, the default setting).
Examples:
get textStyle
set textStyle to italic
set textStyle to bold, underline, extend

225

userLevel

Format:
userLevel <1 | 2 | 3 | 4 | 5>
Action:
Governs user level. Browsing is level 1, typing is 2, painting is 3, authoring is 4, and scripting is 5.
Examples:
get user level
set user level to 5

visible

Format:
visible <true | false>
Action:
Lets you set the visibility of a button, field, or window
Examples:
get the visible of bkgnd button "home"
get the visible of tool window
set the visible of field 1 to false

The hide and show commands let you do the same thing as setting the visible of an object.

wideMargins

Format:
wideMargins <true | false>
Action:
Governs margins of a field
Examples:
get wideMargins
set wideMargins of card field 2 to true   --widens margins of field

System Messages

arrowKey

Format:

on I end I send arrowKey <direction> [to <destination>]

Action:

Traps for or sends message of the keypress of an arrow (cursor) key

Example:

```
on arrowKey right
    go to card "Asia"
end arrowKey right
```

The arrowKey message can be used to substitute for the standard use of the arrow keys, which is navigating from card to card. With arrowKey, you can assign any other function to them. For example, in a stack of maps, arrowUp might move the browser to a card that shows a region north of the map on the current card.

close

Format:

on I end I send close<object type> [to <destination>]

Action:

Traps for and sends message of the closing of objects

Example:

```
on closeStack
    put "Goodbye" into the message box
    wait 2 seconds
end closeStack
```

This stack script flashes a goodbye message for 2 seconds before the stack is closed.

delete

Format:

on I end I send delete<object type> [to <destination>]

Action:

Traps for or sends message of the deletion of a button, field, card, background, or stack

227

Example:
```
on mouseUp
    send deletebutton to bkgnd button "TRex"
end mouseUp
```

This button script sends a deleteButton message to button TRex, making that button disappear.

doMenu

Format:

on I end I pass I send doMenu item [to <destination>]

Action:

Traps for the selection of a menu option

Example:
```
on doMenu anyitem
    if anyitem is "Quit HyperCard" then
        answer "Are You Sure?" with "Cancel" or "OK"
        if it is "OK" then
            quit HyperCard
            else exit doMenu
        end if
        pass doMenu
end doMenu
```

Make sure to include pass doMenu (see the pass command, above) so that doMenu won't trap any additional menu choices.

enterKey

Format:

on I end I send enterKey [to <destination>]

Action:

Traps for or sends message of the keypress of the Enter key

Example:
```
on enterKey
    put field 1 into field 2
end enterKey
```

Hitting the enter key puts the contents of field 1 into field 2.

idle

Format:

on | end | pass | send idle [to <destination>]

Action:

Traps for or sends an idle message

Example:

```
on idle
    subtract 1 from field "Countdown"
    wait 1 second
    pass idle
end idle
```

This script subtracts 1 from the value in the field Countdown every second as long as the script continues to receive an idle message. Be sure to pass idle so that other handlers can receive it as well.

mouseDown

Format:

on | end | send mouseDown [to <destination>]

Action:

Traps for or sends message of the downpress of the mouse button

Example:

```
on mouseDown
    go home
end mouseDown
```

mouseEnter

Format:

on | end | send mouseEnter [to <destination>]

Action:

Traps for or sends message of the entry of the pointer into a defined area, like the boundary of a button or field

Example:

```
on mouseEnter
    go to next card
end mouseEnter
```

This script traps for the entry of the pointer into the area of the object to which the script is attached. The script is triggered as the pointer crosses the object boundary.

229

mouseLeave

Format:

on | end | send mouseLeave [to <destination>]

Action:

Traps for or sends message of the exit of the pointer from a defined area, like the boundary of a button or field.

Example:

```
on mouseLeave
    go to prev card
end mouseLeave
```

This script traps for the exit of the pointer from the area of the object to which the script is attached. The script is triggered as the pointer crosses the object boundary.

mouseStillDown

Format:

on | end | send mouseStillDown [to <destination>]

Action:

Traps for or sends message of the continuing downpress of the mouse button

Example:

```
on mouseStillDown
    play "phaser blast"
    wait 20 clicks
end mouseStillDown
```

This script detects the continued downpress of the mouse button and plays the sound phaser blast at 20-click intervals.

mouseUp

Format:

on | end | send mouseUp [to <destination>]

Action:

Traps for or sends message of the release of the mouse button

Example:
```
on mouseUp
    send mouseUp to card button "Beep Me"
end mouseUp
```

This button script is triggered by a mouseUp message and sends another mouseUp message to a button Beep Me.

mouseWithin

Format:

on | end | send mouseWithin [to <destination>]

Action:

Traps for or sends message that the position of the pointer is within a defined area, like the boundary of a button or field

Example:
```
on mouseWithin
    put "This area is now off limits to humans" into message box
end mouseWithin
```

This button script traps for the continued existence of the pointer within the area of the button. The script is triggered as long as the pointer remains within the button boundary.

new

Format:

on | end | send new<object type> [to <destination>]

Action:

Traps for or sends messages on the creation of new objects

Example:
```
on newCard
    put "Don't forget to add links to this card!" into the message box
end newCard
```

This card script traps for the creation of a new card and puts a reminder in the message box.

open

Format:

on | end open <object type>

Action:

Traps for or sends messages on the opening of an object (usually a field, card, or stack)

Example:

```
on openStack
    put "Hey good buddy!" into the message box
end openStack
```

This stack script puts a greeting into the message box when you open the stack.

quit

Format:

on | end quit [HyperCard]

Action:

Traps for quitting the program

Example:

```
on quit
    go to card "Goodbye to all that"
    wait 3 secs
end quit
```

resume

Format:

on | end resume [HyperCard]

Action:

Traps for for reentering *HyperCard* from another application that was opened from within *HyperCard*

Example:

```
on resume
    getHomeInfo
    pass resume      --to an external command (XCMD),
                     --if present
end resume
```

This script, which is an actual fragment of the *HyperCard* Startup disk Home stack script, is nearly identical to a startup script (see below), and has to perform much the same function. (That's because the startup script procedures are nullified when you launch another application.) The custom command getHomeInfo triggers another part of the script with lengthy instructions for setting up the Home stack and other aspects of the program. After a resume message, you will be returned to the exact place from where you exited *HyperCard*.

returnKey

Format:

on | end | send returnKey

Action:

Traps for the keypress of the Return key

Example:

```
on returnKey
    put field 1 + field 2 into field 3
end returnKey
```

This field script adds the contents of the fields when the return key is pressed.

startUp

Format:

on | end startUp [HyperCard]

Action:

Traps for the startup message when you enter *HyperCard*.

Example:

```
on startUp
    getHomeInfo
    pass startup   --to an external command (XCMD), if present
end startup
```

This startup script, an actual fragment of the *HyperCard* Startup disk Home stack script, triggers the rest of the script when *HyperCard* sends a startup message to the first card of the stack being opened--the Home stack, in this case. The custom command getHomeInfo triggers another part of the script with more detailed startup instructions.

suspend

Format:

on | end suspend [HyperCard]

Action:

Traps for the suspend *HyperCard* message when another application is opened from within *HyperCard*

Example:

```
on suspend
    put "Au revoir" into the message box
    wait 3 secs
end suspend
```

This works much like the quit script above; it puts a goodbye message into the message box as you exit *HyperCard*. In most situations, it isn't necessary to have a message handler for the suspend message; the Home stack, for example, has handlers only for the startUp and resume system messages. Under forthcoming versions of *HyperCard*, however, you may be able to use the suspend message to trigger a script that carries on some *HyperCard* action behind the scenes while another program is in the foreground.

tabKey

Format:

on | end | send tabKey

Action:

Traps for or sends message of the keypress of the Tab key

Example:

```
on tabKey
    doMenu "New Card"
end tabKey
```

This field script could automatically create a new card when the tab key is pressed at the end of data entry on the current card.

Appendices

Appendix A
Importing and Exporting Text and Graphics

One of the best ways to use *HyperCard* is as an information organizer for text and graphics you create with other applications, such as word processors, spreadsheets, and paint programs. Luckily, it's easy to import and export files to and from *HyperCard*.

Graphics

HyperCard can import, create, and export pictures that conform to the standard MacPaint file format. Since most paint programs and clip art collections also use the MacPaint format, moving pictures in and out of *HyperCard* is a snap.

To import pictures:
1. Make sure your graphics program creates *MacPaint* files. Many structured drawing (drafting and CAD) programs, such as *MacDraw,* will not save files in *MacPaint* format unless you specifically ask them to.
2. Align the extreme upper left corner of your picture with the extreme upper left corner of the screen (leaving room for the menu bar), using the scroll bars to get up into the corner if necessary. If you don't do this, you may lose the lower right part of your picture. Also, keep in mind that *HyperCard* can only use that part of the picture that occupies the standard Macintosh screen area. If your picture is bigger than the screen size, you'll have to trim it, shrink it, or break it up into screen-size panels and load each panel onto a separate card. Save your revised version(s).
3. If you're using floppy disk drives, load *HyperCard* in your first drive and insert the disk with your pictures on it in the second drive. Open *HyperCard* and go to the stack you'll be working with.

4. Select a painting tool from the **Tools** menu and **New Card** from the Edit menu. Then choose **Import Paint** from the File menu.
5. *HyperCard* will display a standard Open File dialog box. Select the picture you want to import from your pictures disk and click on Open. The picture will then load into *HyperCard*, usually as an opaque graphics layer.

Another way to import graphics to *HyperCard* is through the Clipboard or Scrapbook. Copy the image into the Clipboard or Scrapbook from your application, load *HyperCard*, and then paste the image onto a card. Several commercially available desk accessories will help you do essentially the same thing. This works with *MacDraw* files and many other programs that generate non-*MacPaint* graphics.

To export pictures:
1. If you're using two floppy disk drives, load *HyperCard* in the first drive and insert a data disk into the second drive.
2. Open *HyperCard* and go to the card that contains the picture you want to export. Keep in mind that *HyperCard* will export the whole screen as a standard *MacPaint* file.
3. Choose a paint tool, then **Export Paint** from the File menu.
4. *HyperCard* will display a standard Save File dialog box asking you to name the picture and to designate the disk and folder in which you want to save it. Save the picture.
5. When you open the picture file with a compatible paint program, you'll see that its upper left corner is aligned with the upper left corner of the screen.

Another way to export graphics from *HyperCard* is through the Clipboard or Scrapbook. Copy the image—it can be part of a card rather than a whole card, as with the method above—into the Clipboard or Scrapbook from *HyperCard*, and then load any application that accepts *MacPaint* files. Next, paste the image into the application. Again, commercially available paint desktop accessories can also perform this trick.
You can also capture a *HyperCard* screen by pressing Command-Shift-3. This will create a picture file named *Screen 0*, which you can then load into a paint program. You can save

up to ten screens in this way (Screen 0–Screen 9) before you have to erase or rename some of them. Note that this screen-shot feature doesn't work if you are pulling down a menu or viewing a dialog box.

Text

Importing and exporting text can be just as easy as moving graphics. As *HyperCard* grows in importance to the Macintosh community, other Macintosh applications, such as word processors, spreadsheets, and conventional databases, will be sold with a built-in utility to import and export text-only files to and from *HyperCard*. Some existing applications already possess this feature (for example, Foxbase 2.0). Until such utilities become more common, however, there are a few techniques to try when you want to move text.

Some *HyperCard* stacks—such as the file index and datebook stacks supplied with *HyperCard*—allow text stored on the Clipboard to be inserted directly into a text field.

To import text:

1. If you are using two floppy disk drives, load *HyperCard* into the first drive and your text data disk into the second drive. The text can be from a word processor or any other program.
2. Open the file that you want to import. Copy the text into the Clipboard in the usual way.
3. Return to the desktop and open *HyperCard*. Go to the stack and card into which you want to paste the text.
4. Position the *I*-beam cursor at the start of the text field and choose Paste from the Edit menu. The text will appear in the field, ready for further editing.
5. As you might guess, this works best if the number of characters in the text that you are trying to import is the same or fewer than the maximum that the text field can display. If the text is larger than the field's capacity, only that part of the text that fits within the field will be displayed. (The rest will transfer, but it won't be visible unless the field is a scrolling field.)

6. Text can also be imported as graphics using the method for other graphics described above. Remember that graphic text cannot be edited the way a text field can.

   Early versions of *HyperCard* did not include Export and Import buttons. If your version of *HyperCard* includes these buttons, you'll probably find using the Import button much easier if you want to do things like strip many numbers from a database or spreadsheet and paste them onto a succession of cards. For that task, use the Import Text button in the Button Ideas stack on the *HyperCard* Ideas disk. This button, which can be pasted onto any card, initiates a script that asks for the pathname of the file to be imported, opens the file, reads the import text into the fields on the card, and creates as many new cards as necessary to reach the end of the file.

   Hint: In designing a card to accept text from a spreadsheet or database, it makes sense to match the size and arrangements of the text fields on the card with those of the fields in the import file. In other words, you'll be most successful with this method if you design your cards to look like the application or report format you are importing.

   You can also export the contents of a *HyperCard* text field via the clipboard.

To export text:

1. If you are using two floppy disk drives, insert *HyperCard* into the first drive and the destination disk into the second drive.
2. Open *HyperCard* and go to the stack, card, and text field from which you want to export text.
3. Copy the text to the Clipboard. Quit *HyperCard* and open the file to which you want to import. Paste in the text in the usual way.

Appendix B
Keyboard Commands

HyperCard provides a keyboard equivalent for many of the program's commands and features. Learning the most-used keyboard shortcuts can considerably speed your work with *HyperCard,* whether you are creating your own stacks or are just browsing. The following lists of the keyboard equivalents are grouped by function.

Navigation Keys

Command	Key	Menu
Back through cards	Down Arrow	
Browse tool	Command-Tab	Tools
Cancel current action	Command-. (period)	
Find (text)	Command-F	Go
First card	Command-1 or	Go
	Command-left arrow	
Forward through retraced cards	Up Arrow	
Help stack	Command-?	Go
Home card	Command-H	Go
Last card	Command-4 or	Go
	Command-Right Arrow	
Message box	Command-M	Go
Next card	Command-3 or	Go
	Right Arrow	
Next field on card	Tab	
Open stack	Command-O	File
Previous card	Command-2 or	Go
	Left Arrow	
Previous field on card	Shift-Tab	
Quit *HyperCard*	Command-Q	File
Recent	Command-R	Go
Store card location	Command-Down Arrow	
Return to stored card	Command-Up Arrow	
Undo	Command-Z	Edit

Text Formatting Keys

Command	Key
Font, next available	Command-Shift->
Font, previous available	Command-Shift-<
Less space between lines	Command-Option-<
More space between lines	Command-Option->
Soft return	Option-Return
Text size, larger	Command->
Text size, smaller	Command-<
Text Style dialog box	Command-T
Undo	Command-Z

Graphics Keys

Note: Most graphics keys work only if a paint tool is selected.

Command	Key
Black pattern in Patterns palette	B
Center (toggle on-off)	C
Darken	D
Clear selection	Backspace
FatBits (toggle on-off)	Option-F, Command-click with Pencil on
FatBits scrolling	Option-drag
Fill	F
Flip horizontal	H
Flip vertical	V
Graphic Text	Command-S
Grid (toggle on-off)	G
Hide/show menu bar	Command-Space bar
Invert	I
Keep	Command-K
Lighten	L
Multiple (toggle on-off)	M
Line widths	1, 2, 3, 4, 6, or 8
Opaque	O
Paste minicard from clipboard	Command-Shift-Y
Patterns palette (toggle on-off)	Tab
Pickup	P
Revert	R
Select	S
Select all	A
Show card picture (paint tool on)	Option-D
Show opaque areas (paint tool on)	Option-O
Spacing between multiples	Option-1 through 8
Tools palette (toggle on-off)	Option-Tab
Trace edges	E
Transparent	T
White pattern in Patterns palette	W
Rotate left	[
Rotate right	]
Undo last action (paint tool on)	~ (tilde)

Graphics Keys (continued)

Tool	Drag w/ Command key	Drag w/ Option key	Drag w/ Shift key
Brush	Erase		Paint horizontally or vertically only
Button	Make new button	Copy button	Move button horizontally or vertically only
Curve		Patterned border	
Eraser	Erase white		Erase horizontally or vertically only
Field	Make new field	Copy field	Move field horizontally or vertically only
Lasso	Lasso all	Copy selection	Move selection horizontally or vertically only
Line		Draw with pattern	Draw 15-degree angles
Oval		Patterned border	Draw circle
Pencil	Toggle in/out of Fatbits		Draw horizontally or vertically only
Polygon		Draw with pattern	Draw 15-degree angles
Rectangle		Patterned border	Draw square
Regular Polygon		Patterned border	Rotate by 15 degrees
Rounded Rectangle		Patterned border	Draw rounded square
Selection	Select close to shape	Copy selection	Move selection horizontally or vertically only
Spray	Erasing spray		Spray horizontally or vertically only

HyperCard Command Keys

Command	Key
Background on-off	Command-B
Bring Closer	Command-+ (plus)
Copy	Command-C
Cut	Command-X
Delete card	Command-Backspace
Find	Command-F
Find again (in scripts only)	Command-G
Find selection (in scripts only)	Command-H
First	Command-1
Help	Command-?
Home	Command-H
Last	Command-4
Message bar on-off	Command-M
New Card	Command-N
Next	Command-3
Open Stack	Command-O
Paste	Command-Y
Previous	Command-2
Print card	Command-P
Quit *HyperCard*	Command-Q
Recent	Command-R
Select	Command-S
Select all	Command-A
Send farther	Command-— (minus)
Show all buttons	Command-Option
Show all fields	Command-Shift-Option
Stop action of script	Command-. (period)
Stop printing	Command-. (period)
Undo	Command-Z

Appendix C
HyperCard Glossary

application
Computer program that helps you accomplish a particular task, such as word processing or graphics.

authoring
Using the *HyperCard* card and stack modifying tools to create your own applications; the fourth *HyperCard* user level. *See also* scripting.

background
The bottom-most layer of a card. The background may include background pictures, background fields, and background buttons, which may be common to many or all cards in a stack.

browse tool
Tool for clicking buttons and searching for text. This is the basic navigation tool in *HyperCard*. It changes from a pointing hand to an *I*-beam when it passes over a text field that you may edit. The menu selection for the Browse tool is in the Tools menu.

browsing
Looking or searching through cards; the most basic *HyperCard* user level.

button
Object that you click on to initiate an action (for example, going to another card). Buttons link cards and stacks together; their actions are defined by HyperTalk scripts. There are two kinds of buttons: card buttons, which are unique to a card, and background buttons, which are inherited by every card with the same background.

button tool
Lets you create and modify buttons. The menu selection for the Button tool is in the Tools menu.

card
The fundamental *HyperCard* unit. It is a full screen of *HyperCard* information—text, graphics, and buttons (links). *See also* stack.

command
Any instruction you issue to *HyperCard* to make it perform an action; specifically, one of the instruction words (such as go and find) included in HyperTalk. Commands can be issued with a menu selection, via the message box, or in a script.

constant
In HyperTalk, a term that substitutes for a predefined value. HyperTalk constants can be used to enter values from the mouse and keyboard, such as down, quote, and tab, or to show whether certain values are true or false.

container
A storage place for *HyperCard* information. These include local and global variables, selected text, messages in the message box, and fields containing text.

control structure
In HyperTalk, a statement that makes a decision or repeats an action with variations until a desired result is obtained.

expression
A mathematical statement or sequence of symbols that has a single value as a solution.

field
Card area where you can type in text. There are two kinds of fields: card fields, which are unique to a card, and background fields, which are inherited by every card with the same background.

field tool
Tool for creating fields. With the field tool and associated menu options, you can make fields of various sizes, shapes, and positions. The field tool is in the Tool menu.

function
In HyperTalk, a word that asks for and retrieves the current state of a *HyperCard* or Macintosh activity. A function returns a result, such as the current time and date or the number of characters in a text field.

general tool
The browse, button, or field tools.

help
HyperCard's online, disk-based assistance stack. Gain access to Help from the Go menu or by clicking on the Help icon in the Home card.

hierarchy
The ladder of *HyperCard* objects. The hierarchy begins at the bottom with buttons and fields and progresses to the card, the background, the stack, the home stack, and finally to *Hyper-Card* itself.

home stack
Index stack to your *HyperCard* stacks. The first card in the Home stack, the Home card, is a "safe place" to begin and end your travels in the program. Go to the Home card by choosing Home from the Go menu.

hypermedia
A form of information organization in which all facts in an information base are cross-referenced to each other and are instantly accessible from any part of the base. *HyperCard* is the first hypermedia application.

hypertalk
HyperCard's programming language. With HyperTalk, you can write scripts for new *HyperCard* applications.

hypertext
Multidimensional text; text cross-referenced by buttons and links to other related text.

layer
The level of a button or field on a card or background. Each button or field is given its own layer when you create it; the topmost layer is the one created last.

link
A connection between cards or stacks. A link is activated by a button, message, or menu selection.

message
A basic HyperTalk communication sent via the message box or a script. Messages are usually commands.

message box
Window in which you can enter a message to communicate with *HyperCard*. Call up the message box by choosing Message from the Go menu.

message handler
Part of a HyperTalk script that looks for and acts on a message. *See also* script.

object
One of the elements of *HyperCard*, such as a button, field, or card. All objects can have scripts attached to them.

operator
In HyperTalk, a mathematical function, such as + (plus), * (multiply), and > (greater than). Operators return a value, such as a sum or the result of a comparison between two numbers.

painting
Using the *HyperCard* graphics tools to create pictures; the third *HyperCard* user level.

palette
A tear-off menu once it has been detached from the menu bar.

pathname
The full name of any Macintosh file, which includes the disk and folder names as well as the file name. Example:

HyperCard Help:Help Stacks:Help Samples.

picture
A *HyperCard* graphic created with the painting tools or imported from another paint program, such as *MacPaint*.

power key
Any key that activates a menu option when a paint tool is selected.

programming language
Artificial system of vocabulary and syntax, often based on a natural language like English, that you can use to "talk" to a computer and to write custom applications. HyperTalk is a programming language. *See also* HyperTalk.

property
Any characteristic of a *HyperCard* object, such as its location. Properties can be *global* (they can be shared by all objects in *HyperCard*), or very *narrow* (the name of a button). *See also* text property.

recent
Dialog box that shows you, in miniature, the 42 most recent cards you have visited. Click on any image of a card to go to it. The Recent menu option is in the Go menu.

script
In HyperTalk, a series of instructions that defines the characteristics, purpose, and action of an object.

scripting
Writing scripts for *HyperCard* objects; the fifth and most advanced *HyperCard* user level.

search path
The route *HyperCard* takes through disks, folders, and files to retrieve requested information. The search path is specified by a pathname, such as HD-20:HyperCard Stacks:MyStack. *See also* pathname.

selection
Any *HyperCard* object that you have most recently created or activated; also, any area you've outlined with the selection or lasso tools in the paint menu.

sound effects
Sounds or music that can be produced by *HyperCard*, usually when you click on a button. Create sounds with HyperTalk's Play command.

stack
A group of related cards. A stack is usually devoted to one theme—a picture catalogue, perhaps—and often all cards in a stack have the same background. A stack can be opened from the Finder just like a document. *See also* card.

stackware
Applications stacks designed by *HyperCard* users.

tear-off menu
A menu that can be detached from the menu bar and positioned anywhere on the screen. *HyperCard*'s Tools and Patterns menus are tear-off menus. *See also* palette.

text
Words typed into a text field or inserted as graphics into a card or background.

text property
The typeface, font, spacing, and alignment of any text.

tool
Device for doing work in *HyperCard*. There are tools for browsing, text editing, painting, and creating buttons and fields. *See also* general tool.

typing
Act of entering text into a text field or the message box; the
second *HyperCard* user level.

user level
One of five settings that determines what *HyperCard* tools and
features will be available to the user. The five settings—
browsing, typing, painting, authoring, and scripting—give pro-
gressively greater control to the user. Set your user preference
with the user preference card in the Home stack.

variable
A temporary container for *HyperCard* information. Variables
can be *local*, active only for the duration of the current message handler, or they can be *global*, active until you specifically eliminate them.

visual effects
Visual transitions from one card to the next. These include
various kinds of cinematic zooms, dissolves, and wipes.
HyperCard can also do simple two-dimensional animation.

Index

COMPUTE! Books

Ask your retailer for these **COMPUTE! Books** or order directly from **COMPUTE!**.

Write COMPUTE! Books, F.D.R. Station, P.O. Box 5038, New York, NY 10150.

Quantity	Title	Price*	Total
_____	Mastering *Microsoft Word* on the Macintosh (118-8)	$18.95	_____
_____	COMPUTE!'s Quick and Easy Guide to *Excel* on the Mac (131-5)	$10.95	_____
_____	COMPUTE!'s Quick & Easy Guide to *Word* on the Mac (135-8)	$10.95	_____
_____	Making Dollars and Cents with *Dollars and Sense* (101-3)	$18.95	_____
_____	Mastering *MacDraw* (102-1)	$18.95	_____
_____	Becoming a MacArtist (80-9)	$18.95	_____
_____	MacTalk: Telecomputing on the Macintosh (85-X)	$16.95	_____
_____	MacOffice: Using the Macintosh for Everything (006)	$19.95	_____
_____	MacIdeas (015-7)	$16.95	_____
_____	Using Your Macintosh: Beginning Microsoft BASIC and Applications (021-1)	$17.95	_____
_____	Advanced Macintosh BASIC Programming (030-0)	$18.95	_____
_____	MacBits: Utilities and Routines for the BASIC Programmer (075-0)	$18.95	_____
_____	Mastering *Microsoft Works* (042-4)	$17.95	_____

*Add $2.00 per book for shipping and handling.
Outside US add $5.00 air mail or $2.00 surface mail.

NC residents add 5% sales tax _____
NY residents add 8.25% sales tax _____
Shipping & handling: $2.00/book _____
Total payment _____

All orders must be prepaid (check, charge, or money order).
All payments must be in US funds.
☐ Payment enclosed.
Charge   ☐ Visa   ☐ MasterCard   ☐ American Express

Acct. No._____ Exp. Date _____
                                                   (Required)
Name _____

Address _____

City_____ State _____ Zip _____

*Allow 4–5 weeks for delivery.
Prices and availability subject to change.
Current catalog available upon request.